Dec. 2005

the
wabi-sabi
house

# the wabi-sabi house

the
Japanese
art
of imperfect
beauty

ROBYN GRIGGS LAWRENCE

PHOTOGRAPHS BY JOE COCA

CLARKSON POTTER/PUBLISHERS
NEW YORK

Grateful acknowledgment is made to the Freer Gallery of Art and
Arthur M. Sackler Gallery Archives at the Smithsonian Institution,
Washington, D.C., for permission to reprint excerpts from
The Elizabeth Gordon Papers. Gift of Elizabeth Gordon, 1988.

Excerpts reprinted from *The Unknown Craftsman* by Soetsu Yanagi,
adapted by Bernard Leach, copyright © 1972, 1989 with permission
from Kodansha International.

Copyright © 2004 by Robyn Griggs Lawrence
All rights reserved. No part of this book may be reproduced or transmitted in
any form or by any means, electronic or mechanical, including photocopying,
recording, or by any information storage and retrieval system, without permission in writing from the publisher.

Published by Clarkson Potter/Publishers, New York, New York
Member of the Crown Publishing Group, a division of Random House, Inc.
www.crownpublishing.com

CLARKSON N. POTTER is a trademark and POTTER and colophon are reg-
istered trademarks of Random House, Inc.

Printed in the United States of America

Design by Maggie Hinders

Library of Congress Cataloging-in-Publication Data
Lawrence, Robyn Griggs.
        The Wabi-Sabi house: the Japanese art of imperfect beauty / Robyn
Griggs Lawrence.
1. Interior decoration—psychological aspects.   2. Zen Buddhism—Influence.
3. Decoration and ornament—Japan—Themes, motives.
I. Title. NK2113.L39   2004
747'.0952—dc22    2003027601

ISBN 1-4000-5046-4

10  9  8  7  6  5  4  3  2  1

First Edition

*For My Father*

*Just as I was finishing this book, my father, Carrol Griggs,*

*succumbed to a long, tough battle with cancer. He was the man*

*who taught me the value of fine craftsmanship and awoke in me*

*an eye for simple, clean design. But far more important, my dad*

*instilled in me a pure appreciation for home. He reveled in the*

*elegant, epicurean pleasures of hearth and family, and he showed*

*me that everything I'll ever need can be found within.*

| wabi-sabi is... | wabi-sabi isn't... |
|---|---|
| dry leaves | cherry blossoms |
| bare branches | floral arrangements |
| handmade | machine made |
| weathered wood | plastic laminate |
| crumbling stone | polished marble |
| wildflowers | roses |
| wool | polyester |
| rice paper | plate glass |
| clay | china |
| unbleached cotton | cashmere |
| tea | latte |
| vintage | designer |
| cobblestones | concrete |
| adobe | steel |
| arts and crafts | rococo |
| flea markets | warehouse stores |
| salvaged | made to order |
| burlap | velvet |
| oil finish | polyurethane |
| recycled glass | crystal |
| native landscaping | kentucky bluegrass |
| natural linoleum | vinyl |
| hemp | silk |
| clean | cluttered |
| frank lloyd wright | ludwig mies van der rohe |
| natural plaster | drywall |
| natural light | fluorescent light |
| clotheslines | electric dryers |
| hand mixers | food processors |
| rust | dirt |

# Contents

# introduction

The essence of education is not to transfer knowledge; it is to guide the learning process, to put responsibility for study into the students' own hands. It is not the piecemeal merchandising of information; it is the bestowal of keys that allow people to unlock the vault of knowledge on their own. It does not consist of pilfering the intellectual property amassed by others through no additional effort of one's own; it would rather place people on their own path of discovery and invention.

—EDUCATOR AND AUTHOR
TSUNESABURO MAKIGUCHI

Several years ago, I was on assignment in rural Maine, looking for houses to feature in *Natural Home* magazine. I landed at a sweetly rustic stone house on a hillside, built completely by hand and appointed with cozy flea market furniture and other Dumpster finds. The stove was vintage 1930s, with narrow rivulets of rust in the chipped and yellowing enamel. The wooden dining chairs didn't match, and the wine-colored overstuffed chair near the woodstove carried the slightly soiled chic of a bygone era. Kate, the homeowner, told me about her seasonal lifestyle: summers spent growing vegetables, fruit, and herbs; falls spent canning and preserving; winters huddled in that cozy chair pulled up close to the fire. We discussed her casual yet careful decorating style; nothing was new, but everything had a story behind it and a reason for being in her home. At one point, I asked about a rusty grate hanging on the wall.

"Oh, that," she said. "That is *so wabi-sabi*."

"Wobby *what?*" I asked.

She described wabi-sabi as the Japanese art of appreciating the imperfect, the primitive, the incomplete, and she sent me home with a slim volume, *Wabi-Sabi for Artists, Designers, Poets and Philosophers*, by Leonard Koren—one of the most important gifts

9

I've ever received. Before I even read Koren's book, I knew that I'd been wabi-sabi all my life. But now I could point to something concrete when answering to my mother, my husband, and assorted others about my wild garden, the raw-wood salvaged french doors that I refused to paint, the enamel Depression-era table I use as a desk. I set out to learn everything I possibly could about this concept, and my outlook expanded dramatically in the process.

While chipping paint, distressed wood, and rust—the patina of graceful aging—are important parts of the wabi-sabi aesthetic, wabi-sabi is so much more than a "look" you can incorporate into your home, like French country or shabby chic. *Wabi* began as a literary concept, reflected in melancholy Japanese poetry during the fifth and sixth centuries. It emerged as an important cultural barometer when Tea Master Sen no Rikyu brought *chanoyu*, known by many as the tea ceremony, to the Japanese masses in the sixteenth century. *Sabi* became more important in Japan in the seventeenth century, when the warlords embraced tea, and the two concepts have been inextricably bound together ever since. Intimately tied to Zen Buddhism, wabi-sabi carries a subtle spiritual component, reminding us that home should be a sanctuary, not a loud place full of disturbance and distraction. To create serenity at home, wabi-sabi asks that we set aside our judgments and our longing for perfection and focus, instead, on the beauty of things as they are, at this very moment.

Wabi-sabi encompasses lifestyle elements that are crucial in a society where no one has time to think and everyone wants it yesterday. Threads of the ancient wabi-sabi mentality remain as an undercurrent in modern Japan, despite the teeming, techno-hurried, sleep-deprived mood that pervades its cities.' Rather than tossing purchases into a bag, store clerks wrap them in paper, transforming them into a small moment of celebration. Even the simplest meals are a visual feast,' artfully arranged to honor the food as well as the dishes and utensils used to serve it. When I found myself hopelessly lost on the twisted alleyways of old Asakusa in Tokyo, several people stopped, and one couple actually walked me to my destination.

The subtle messages that live within wabi-sabi are the things we all seem to long for today: Slow down. Take the time to find beauty in what seems ordinary—and to turn the "ordinary" into something beautiful. Make things yourself instead of buying those spit out by a machine,' and smile when your work is flawed. Wash your dishes by hand.* And, most important, I believe: learn to think of others before yourself.

In my research on wabi-sabi, I've run into people—both here and in Japan—who say Americans will never, ever get this thing. We're too materialistic, they say, too enamored of the pursuit of stuff. We're afraid of real decay and poverty; we'll simply equate wabi-sabi with a rustic "look" and try to make a buck off it, sacrificing authenticity for immediacy.

There's some truth to all of that, of course, and the stereotypes weren't born without our help. During the post–World War II occupation, many of the Americans who requisitioned Japanese houses painted the woodwork to "brighten" the subdued harmonies of buildings—to the horror of the homeowners. In the late 1950s, American tourists oohed and aahed when the Golden Pavilion in

Kyoto was rebuilt with dazzling gilded walls. The people of Kyoto were less impressed. "Wait ten years," they said. "Wait until it acquires some patina."

Soetsu Yanagi, father of the craft movement in mid-twentieth-century Japan, believed no one could truly comprehend wabi in his day and age, so he used the related term *shibui* (literally "severe good taste"), which people were more familiar with. In 1960, *House Beautiful* editor Elizabeth Gordon became enamored of shibui and published two special issues devoted to it. A few years ago, I spent a day at the Freer-Sackler Gallery in Washington, D.C., reading through the box of fan mail these issues generated. "*House Beautiful* has never had so deep a response to an issue from so many people," Gordon stated—and it probably hasn't since.

Amid those letters, I found one from Hatsuko Ashihara, which read: "We are very much surprised to see picking up the phase of our culture which we had believed you Americans could never understand." I noticed she didn't say "pleased"; she said "surprised." As many Japanese have pointed out to me, they are often quite directly indirect in their communication.

There's inherent danger in attempting to translate any concept across cultures, especially from East to West (or vice versa). In the course of this book, I'll take great liberties with a Japanese philosophy, bringing to it my own Western-rooted predilections and belief system. In attempting to translate a centuries-old concept for a twenty-first-century audience, I'll address issues the ancient Zen masters might have found ludicrous. Soundproofing? Modernism? There was simply no context for these in fifteenth-century Japan.

12

If we were to be truly authentic and never veer from wabi-sabi's original tenets, not one of us would ever be able to invite the concept into our lives, and that would be a shame. What I'm hoping to convey in this book is not a didactic system with a bunch of rules and regulations, but a spirit. And I believe it's a spirit that lives in us all—if we're willing to let it breathe.

Many people I met with in Japan were thrilled that I was attempting to bring wabi-sabi to Westerners. Some smiled gently when I mentioned my research; one woman even giggled. "Wabi-sabi is very difficult, even for us to understand," she said. "No other word could be more ambiguous in meaning than wabi," Kazue Kyoichi wrote in *Wabicha no Keifu* in 1973. "It's impossible to explain in other words." For this reason, many Japanese attempt to explain it by example, illustration, and metaphor.

Everyone has a slightly different definition of wabi-sabi and usually a personal agenda toward how it should be explained and incorporated into people's lives. Attempting to unfold the many layers of wabi-sabi will be a lifelong process for me, fascinating and at times completely frustrating. The more I learn, the more I realize I have to learn. My first impression—that wabi-sabi is everything today's sleek, mass-produced, technology-saturated culture isn't—was eventually revealed as superficial. Over lunch in Tokyo, art critic, producer, and tea practitioner Junji Ito told me he had used the words in the title of a museum exhibition on robots, a nod to wabi-sabi's animistic worldview, which endows everything (even robots) with spirit. I traveled out to the ancient pottery center of

Shigaraki to visit Buddhist priest Shiho Kanzaki, whose superb vases, pots, and tea bowls, fired in traditional wood-fired Anagama kilns, embody the very essence of wabi-sabi not only in form but also in function. We talked less about the aesthetics of pottery and more about the nature of its inspiration. "Manner and behavior is most important," he told me. "You always have to think of other persons. If you are always thinking of other persons, you can understand the real wabi-sabi."

This was the piece I hadn't anticipated—and the aspect of Japanese culture that I fell most in love with. I learned that the same character used to write *tsukaeru,* to be of service to one another, can also be read as *shiawase,* or happiness. I learned to turn to the person next to me before drinking during a tea gathering and say, "Excuse me for going before you." I learned to bring a gift when someone is kind enough to meet with me and to present it with reverence. I learned that when guests take off their shoes upon entering my home, turning the shoes around to face the door will make them easier to slip into when it's time to leave.

These are the intangibles, the small daily acts that have nothing to do with decorating, organizing your living space, or embracing imperfection. Yet these are the wabi-sabi lessons that can make a home happier and more peaceful. These acts can be as simple as offering everyone who stops by a cup of tea, and serving it with cookies. Garnishing the dinner plate with a few sprigs of fresh basil. Replacing the roll of toilet paper after you use the last sheet. For years, incensed that my husband throws inside-out clothes into the laundry, I've sloppily folded them with the seams still on the outside. My new wabi-sabi consideration asks me to rethink that. (Of course, I do harbor hope that some day he realizes how helpful it would be to turn them outside out in the first place . . .)

In this book, I will talk about uncluttering, seeking out salvage and flea market finds, quieting your house, and learning to let go of our media-driven need for "the perfect home." All of these will help bring vestiges of the harmony and peace we're seeking through wabi-sabi—but none is paramount. Whether you come to eschew the neon green plastic wastebasket and learn to weave your own out of willow boughs—or not—I hope you'll keep Kanzaki-san's words at the top of your mind: all you really have to remember is to be considerate of others.

Let your wabi-sabi life begin.

15

# what is wabi-sabi?

# think

Pared down to its barest essence, wabi-sabi is the Japanese art of finding beauty in imperfection and profundity in nature, of <u>accepting</u> the natural cycle of growth, decay, and death. It's simple, slow, and uncluttered—and it reveres authenticity above all. Wabi-sabi is flea markets, not warehouse stores; aged wood, not Pergo; rice paper, not glass. It celebrates cracks and crevices and all the other marks that time, weather, and loving use leave behind. It reminds us that we are all but transient beings on this planet—that our bodies as well as the material world around us are in the process of returning to the dust from which we came. Through wabi-sabi, we learn to embrace liver spots, rust, and frayed edges, and the march of time they represent.

The Japanese view of life embraced a simple aesthetic that grew stronger as inessentials were eliminated and trimmed away.

—ARCHITECT TADAO ANDO

17

Wabi-sabi is underplayed and modest, the kind of quiet, unde-clared beauty that waits patiently to be discovered. It's a fragmentary glimpse: the branch representing the entire tree, shoji screens filtering the sun, the moon 90 percent obscured behind a ribbon of cloud. It's a richly mellow beauty that's striking but not obvious, that you can imagine having around you for a long, long time—Katharine Hepburn versus Marilyn Monroe. For the Japanese, it's the difference between *kirei*—merely "pretty"—and *omoshiroi,* the interestingness that kicks something into the realm of beautiful. (Omoshiroi literally means "white faced," but its meanings range from fascinating to fantastic.) It's the peace found in a moss garden, the musty smell of geraniums, the astringent taste of powdered green tea. My favorite Japanese phrase for describing wabi-sabi is *natsukashii furusato,* or an old memory of my hometown. (This is a prevalent mind-set in Japan these days, as people born in major urban areas such as Tokyo and Osaka wax nostalgic over grandparents' country houses that perhaps never were. They can even "rent" grandparents who live in prototypical country houses and spend the weekend there.)

Daisetz T. Suzuki, who was one of Japan's foremost English-speaking authorities on Zen Buddhism and one of the first scholars to interpret Japanese culture for Westerners, described wabi-sabi as "an active aesthetical appreciation of poverty." He was referring to poverty not as we in the West interpret—and fear—it but in the more romantic sense of removing the huge weight of material concerns from our lives. "Wabi is to be satisfied with a little hut, a room of two or three tatami mats, like the log cabin of Thoreau," he wrote, "and with a dish of vegetables picked in the neighboring fields, and perhaps to be listening to the pattering of a gentle spring rainfall."

In Japan, there is a marked difference between a Thoreau-like *wabibito* (wabi person), who is free in his heart, and a *makoto no hinjin*, a more Dickensian character whose poor circumstances make him desperate and pitiful. The ability to make do with less is revered; I heard someone refer to a wabibito as a person who could make something complete out of eight parts when most of us would use ten. For us in the West, this might mean choosing a smaller house or a smaller car, or—just as a means of getting started—refusing to supersize our fries.

The words *wabi* and *sabi* were not always linked, although they've been together for such a long time that many people (including D. T. Suzuki) use them interchangeably. One tea teacher I talked with begged me not to use the phrase *wabi-sabi* because she believes the marriage dilutes their separate identities; a tea master in Kyoto laughed and said they're thrown together because it sounds catchy, kind of like Ping-Pong. In fact, the two words do have distinct meanings, although most people don't fully agree on what they might be.

Wabi stems from the root *wa*, which refers to harmony, peace, tranquillity, and balance. Generally speaking, wabi had the original meaning of sad, desolate, and lonely, but poetically it has come to

19

Enduring poverty in life
I prepare a fire on the
hearth and enjoy the
profound touch of Tea.

—POET MATSUO BASHŌ

✳mean simple, unmaterialistic, humble by choice, and in tune with nature. Someone who is perfectly herself and never craves to be anything else would be described as wabi. Sixteenth-century tea master Jo-o described a wabi tea man as someone who feels no dissatisfaction even though he owns no Chinese utensils with which to conduct tea. A common phrase used in conjunction with wabi is "the joy of the little monk in his wind-torn robe."✳A wabi person epitomizes Zen, which is to say, he or she is content with very little; free from greed, indolence, and anger; and understands the wisdom of rocks and grasshoppers.

Until the fourteenth century, when Japanese society came to admire monks and hermits for their spiritual asceticism, wabi was a pejorative term used to describe cheerless, miserable outcasts. Even today, undertones of desolation and abandonment cling to the word, sometimes used to describe the helpless feeling you have when waiting for your lover. It also carries a hint of dissatisfaction in its underhanded criticism of gaud and ostentation—the defining mark of the ruling classes when *wabisuki* (a taste for all things wabi) exploded in the sixteenth century. In a country ruled by warlords who were expected to be conspicuous consumers, wabi became known as "the aesthetic of the people"—the lifestyle of the everday samurai, who had little in the way of material comforts.

Things fall apart; the center cannot hold.

—W. B. YEATS

✳Sabi by itself means "the bloom of time." It connotes natural progression—tarnish, hoariness, rust—the extinguished gloss of that

20

which once sparkled. It's the understanding that beauty is fleeting. The word's meaning has changed over time, from its ancient definition, "to be desolate," to the more neutral "to grow old." By the thirteenth century, sabi's meaning had evolved into taking pleasure in things that were old and faded. A proverb emerged: "Time is kind to things, but unkind to man."

Sabi things carry the burden of their years with dignity and grace: the chilly mottled surface of an oxidized silver bowl, the yielding gray of weathered wood, the elegant withering of a bereft autumn bough. An old car left in a field to rust, as it transforms from an eyesore into a part of the landscape, could be considered America's contribution to the evolution of sabi. An abandoned barn, as it collapses in on itself, holds this mystique.

There's an aching poetry in things that carry this patina, and it transcends the Japanese. We Americans are ineffably drawn to old European towns with their crooked cobblestone streets and chipping plaster, to places battle scarred with history much deeper than our own. We seek sabi in antiques and even try to manufacture it in distressed furnishings. True sabi cannot be acquired, however. It is a gift of time.

Natural materials, vulnerable to weathering, warping, cracking, and peeling, take on the patina of sabi over time.

# annica

## A KEY TO SABI

During his last weeks, as cancer ate away at his body, I saw my dad grow softer, gentler, and more forgiving. He hugged people readily—not something he'd ever been known to do before. He was grateful for every minute he had left, but he wasn't willing to extend those minutes through painful, invasive medical procedures. He'd accepted that he was going to die, and he was done fighting it. He was more peaceful than he'd ever been.

My dad had come to terms with something that Buddhists call *annica*, the law of impermanence. On his own deathbed, it is said, the Buddha reminded his disciple Ananda that decay is inherent in all physical beings—that death is simply part of the natural order of things. Accepting this inevitability and letting go of our fierce attachment to living allows us to reach *satori*, or enlightenment.

Annica is the core concept behind sabi. Why is it that so many of us find serenity—and aching beauty—in crumbling, rusty, fraying things? By celebrating their decay, we allow ourselves to acknowledge that things do crumble and rust and fray—that they're impermanent. We're tapping into and internalizing life's birth-death-decay cycle, one that our society so often wants to ignore or sanitize. Sabi, then, represents a material manifestation of a key spiritual concept.

Long life is not gained from wealth.

Nor is old age banished by property.

For brief is this life, the wise say,

Non-eternal, subject to change.

—BUDDHA,
FROM THE PALI CANON

So now we have wabi, which is humble and simple, and sabi, which is rusty and weathered. And we've thrown these terms together into a phrase that rolls off the tongue like Ping-Pong. Does that mean, then, that the wabi-sabi house is full of things that are humble, plain, rusty, and weathered? That's the easy answer. The amalgamation of wabi and sabi in practice, however, takes on much more depth.

In home decor, wabi-sabi inspires a minimalism that celebrates the human rather than the machine. Possessions are pared down, and pared down again, until only those that are necessary for their utility or beauty (and ideally both) are left. What makes the cut? Items that you both admire and love to use, like those hand-crank eggbeaters that still work just fine. Things that resonate with the spirit of their makers' hands and hearts: the chair your grandfather made, your six-year-old's lumpy pottery, an afghan you knitted yourself (out of handspun sheep's wool, perhaps). Pieces of your own history: sepia-toned ancestral photos, baby shoes, the Nancy Drew mysteries you read over and over again as a kid.

Wabi-sabi interiors tend to be muted, dimly lit, and shadowy—giving the rooms an enveloping, womblike feeling. Natural materials that are vulnerable to weathering, warping, shrinking, cracking, and peeling lend an air of perishability. The palette is drawn from browns, blacks, grays, earthy greens, and rusts. This implies a lack of freedom but actually affords an opportunity for innovation and creativity. In Japan, kimonos come in a hundred different shades of gray. You simply have to hone your vision so you can see, and feel, them all.

The peculiar dilemma of Americans is not that we have everything, but that when it comes to designing our homes, we can do anything we want. ✳. From the American house emanates a restless and temporary quality, and all too often its interior spaces have an arbitrary quality that is disquieting.

—ANTHONY WEST, IN *HOUSE BEAUTIFUL*, 1960

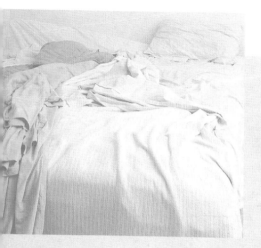

## WABI, NOT SLOBBY

Wabi-sabi can be exploited in all sorts of ways, and one of the most tempting is to use it as an excuse to shrug off an unmade bed, an unswept floor, or a soiled sofa. "Oh, *that*. Well, that's just wabi-sabi." My nine-year-old son, Stacey, loves this tactic.

How tempting it might be to let the split running down the sofa cushion seam continue on its merry way, calling it wabi-sabi. To spend Saturday afternoon at the movies and let the dust settle into the rugs: wabi-sabi. To buy five extra minutes of sleep every morning by not making the bed—as a wabi-sabi statement, of course. And how do you know when you've gone too far—when you've crossed over from simple, serene, and rustic to *überdistress*?

A solid yellow line separates tattered and shabby, dust and dirt from something worthy of veneration. Wabi-sabi is never messy or slovenly. Worn things take on their magic only in settings where it's clear they don't harbor bugs or grime. One senses that they've survived to bear the marks of time precisely because they've been so well cared for throughout the years. Even the most rare and expensive of antiques will never play well in a house that's cluttered or dirty.

Cleanliness implies respect. Both ancient and modern tea masters teach that even the poorest wabi tea person should always use fresh green bamboo utensils and new white cloths for wiping the tea bowl. In tea, the host's cleanliness is considered a clear indicator of his state of mind and his devotion to the way of tea. *Chanoyu Ichieshu*, a tea textbook published in 1956, even goes so far as to advise guests to look into the host's toilet if they wish to understand his spiritual training.

I'm definitely not advocating this extreme. In fact, I'm mortified at the thought of anyone judging me on the state of my own toilets. But the tea masters' point is valid: Spaces that have been thoroughly and lovingly cleaned are ultimately more welcoming. When the bed is neatly made, the romance of a frayed quilt blossoms. The character imparted by a wood floor's knots and crevices shines through when the crumbs are swept away. A scrubbed but faded kilim, thrown over a sofa that's seen one too many stains, transforms it into an irresistible place to rest.

I draw water
I carry wood
This is my magic.

—ZEN POEM

26

Wabi-sabi's roots lie in Zen Buddhism, which was brought from China to Japan by Eisai, a twelfth-century monk. Zen, with its principles of vast emptiness and nothing holy, stresses austerity, communion with nature, and above all, reverence for everyday life as the real path to enlightenment. To reach enlightenment, Zen monks lived ascetic, often isolated lives and sat for long periods of concentrated meditation.

To help his fellow monks stay awake during these excruciating meditation sessions, Eisai taught them how to process tea leaves into a hot drink. Once Eisai was gone, though, tea took on a very different life of its own. Around the fourteenth century, the upper classes developed elaborate rituals involving tea. Large tearooms were built in an ostentatious style known as *shoin,* with numerous Chinese hanging scrolls and a formal arrangement of tables for flower vases and incense burners. Tea practitioners proved their wealth and status through their collections of elegant Chinese-style tea utensils during three-day weekenders where up to one hundred cups of tea—as well as food and sake—were served.

Then along came Murata Shuko, an influential tea master who also happened to be a Zen monk. In a radical fashion departure, Shuko began using understated, locally produced utensils during his tea gatherings. Saying "it is good to tie a praised horse to a straw-thatched house," he combined rough, plain wares with famed Chinese utensils, and the striking contrast made both look more interesting. Shuko's successor, Jo-o, was even more critical of men whose zeal for rare or famed utensils was their main motivation for conducting tea. Jo-o began using everyday items such as the *mentsu*, a wooden pilgrim's eating bowl, as a wastewater container, and a Shigaraki *onioke*, a stoneware bucket used in silk dyeing, as a water jar. He brought unadorned celadon and Korean peasant wares into the tearoom.

It was Jo-o's disciple Sen no Rikyu, however, who is widely credited with establishing the quiet, simple ceremony that made it possible for everyone—not just the wealthy—to practice tea. In the sixteenth century—the beginning of an age of peace following several long centuries of civil war in Japan—gaudiness was all the rage, and Rikyu's tea became an oasis of quiet, simple taste. He served tea in bowls made by anonymous Korean potters and indigenous Japanese craftsmen, the most famous of which are the Raku family's style. He created tiny tea huts (one and a half tatami mats, as opposed to the four-and-one-half- to eighteen-mat rooms that had been the norm) based on the traditional farmer's hut of rough mud walls, a thatched roof, and organically shaped exposed wood structural elements. The hut included a *nijiriguchi*, a low entryway that forced guests to bow and experience humility as they entered. Rikyu made some of his own utensils of unlacquered bamboo (as common as crabgrass in Japan, but nowadays a Rikyu original is worth as much as a Leonardo da Vinci painting), and he arranged flowers simply and naturally in bamboo vases (*shakuhachi*) and baskets. Rikyu's ceremony became known as *wabichado* (*chado* means "the way of tea"), and it endures in Japan to this day.

# shaza kissa

## WABI-SABI AND THE WAY OF TEA

We Westerners tend to scratch our heads at the thought of four hours spent sitting on our knees, participating in an elaborate ritual during which a charcoal fire is built, a meal of seasonal delicacies is served with sake, one bowl of green tea is made and shared among the guests, and then individual bowls of frothy thin tea are made by whisking hot water and *matcha*. What most of us don't realize, however, is that tea embodies so much of the beauty that makes up Japanese culture. To truly understand tea, you must also study poetry, art, literature, architecture, legacy, and history. Tea practitioners are accomplished in the arts of flowers, fine cuisine, and—perhaps most important—etiquette (*sarei*). And the four principles of tea—harmony (*wa*), respect (*kei*), purity (*sei*), and tranquillity (*jaku*)—could of course be the means to any good life.

Tea, in its current form, was born out of a medieval society rife with terrible warfare, yet the samurai were willing to set aside their rank—and their swords—to become equals within the tearoom. The room's design is deliberately simple and clean; it's meant to be a sanctuary. "In this thatched hut there ought not to be a speck of dust of any kind; both master and visitors are expected to be on terms of absolute sincerity; no ordinary measures of proportion or etiquette or conventionalism are to be followed," declares *Nanbo-roku*, one of most ancient and important textbooks on tea. "A fire is made, water is boiled, and tea is served; this is all that is needed here, no other worldly considerations are to intrude." As soon as we enter the tearoom,

The art of *chanoyu* consists in nothing else but in boiling water, making tea, and sipping it.

—TEA MASTER
SEN NO RIKYU

we're asked to shake off our woes and worries and connect with others, "face harmonious, words loving."

* * *

"Tea brings people together in a nonthreatening place to escape the modern world, then they can go back out and take that with them," Gary Cadwallader, an American-born tea master who teaches at the Urasenke Center in Kyoto, explained to me. It seems to me that we Americans who lack the time—or the desire—to learn tea could take the essence of that statement and apply it to our own lives.

"If a friend visits you, make him tea, wish him welcome warmly with hospitality," Jo-o, one of Japan's earliest tea masters, wrote. "Set some flowers and make him feel comfortable." This is embodied in a common Japanese phrase, *shaza kissa*, which translates, "Well, sit down and have some tea." What if we adopted that phrase and learned to say it more often—when the kids get home from school (before the rush to hockey and ballet), when our neighbor stops by, when we feel our annoyance level with our spouse starting to rise? If we just allowed ourselves to stop for a moment, sit down together, and share a cup of tea, what might that moment bring?

In learning tea, we're constantly reminded that every meeting is a once-in-a-lifetime occasion to enjoy good company, beautiful art, and a cup of tea. We never know what might happen tomorrow, or even later today. Stopping whatever it is that's so important (dishes, bill paying, work deadlines) to share conversation and a cup of tea with someone you love—or might love—is an easy opportunity to promote peace. It is from this place of peace, harmony, and fellowship that the true wabi-sabi spirit emerges.

## THE TEN VIRTUES OF TEA

When the Zen monk Eisai brought tea seeds from China to Japan in the twelfth century, he also imparted the following ten virtues of tea.

- ⚘ It has the blessing of all deities.
- ⚘ It promotes filial piety.
- ⚘ It drives away evil spirits.
- ⚘ It banishes drowsiness.
- ⚘ It keeps the five internal organs in harmony.
- ⚘ It wards off disease.
- ⚘ It strengthens friendship.
- ⚘ It disciplines body and mind.
- ⚘ It destroys all passions.
- ⚘ It gives a peaceful death.

Kind of makes you want to switch from coffee, doesn't it?

*Shaza kissa*, which means, "Well, sit down and have some tea," is a commonly heard phrase in Japan. Stopping each day to make and enjoy a pot of tea is a means of connecting to the four principles of the ancient tea ceremony—harmony, respect, purity, and tranquillity—and bringing them into our daily lives.

Wabi-sabi is not a decorating "style" but rather a mind-set. There's no list of rules; we can't hang crystals or move our beds and wait for peace to befall us. Creating a wabi-sabi home is the direct result of developing our *wabigokoro*, or wabi mind and heart: living modestly, learning to be satisfied with life as it can be once we strip away the unnecessary, living in the moment. You see? Simple as that.

This is tough in any culture, of course, but darned near impossible in our own. In America we're plied daily with sales pitches that will help us improve ourselves, our circumstances, our homes. We can have the whitest teeth, the cleanest carpets, and the biggest SUV money can buy.

All of this flies in the face of wabigokoro, as described in Rikyu's sacred tea text, *Nanbo-roku.* "A luxurious house and the taste of delicacies are only pleasures of the mundane world," he wrote. "It is enough if the house does not leak and the food keeps hunger away. This is the teaching of the Buddha—the true meaning of chado."

This is un-American. Or is it? I believe there exists in all of us a longing for something deeper than the whitest teeth, sparkling floors, and eight cylinders. What if we *could* learn to be content with our lives, exactly as they are today? It's a lofty thought . . . but one that's certainly worth entertaining.

You can start cultivating this mind-set in small ways, taking a lesson from tea. In learning to conduct tea, we're taught to handle every utensil, from the bamboo water scoop to the tea bowl, as if it were precious, with the same respect and care we would use to handle a rare antique. You can do the same thing with the items you use every day.

In understanding beauty, intuition is more of the essence than intellectual perception.

—SOETSU YANAGI

31

Start with your coffee or tea mug—the container holding whatever beverage you use to launch your day. If you're using something plastic, or a mug advertising an excavation company, stop. Replace it with pottery that feels solid and heavy in your hand. Invest in the mug—not just monetarily, but with your time. Spend five minutes each morning admiring its shape, its texture, its colors. Try to find something new in that mug every day—something that escaped your purview yesterday. This will open your sensitivity to everything around you: the seasons, the effects of light, the expression on the faces of those you come in contact with.

Christy Bartlett, a San Francisco–based tea master who represents the family of Rikyu's descendants, told me that she does this exercise every morning with a tea bowl that she's had for twenty-two years. "Every time I look at it, I still see something new," she said. But to do this, she warned, "You can't be lazy. It's up to you to see and see something new, to sustain your interest in the world around you. It's not up to the world to entertain you. It requires effort to be interested."

Over sushi in a Kyoto restaurant, Gary Cadwallader assured me that it's not impossible for Westerners to cultivate this kind of interest. Visit museums, he advised, and learn how to shop with an eye for color, texture, and patina. "You can get a grater for a few hundred yen or you can get a more expensive one of copper," Gary said. "But the copper one will last long enough for your great-grandchildren to use. If we use high-quality

Artifacts picked up during your travels are more fun to use than something you've ordered from a catalog. These hand-carved wooden bowls are from Haiti; the bark cloth was obtained in New Guinea in the 1930s. The coffee mug was handmade by a friend.

## SEN NO RIKYU'S SEVEN RULES OF TEA

- ¬ Arrange the flowers as they are in the fields.
- ¬ Lay the charcoal so it boils the water.
- ¬ Create a cool feeling in summer.
- ¬ Make sure the guests are warm in winter.
- ¬ Be sure everything is ready ahead of time and do not fall behind.
- ¬ Be prepared for rain even if it is not raining.
- ¬ Always be mindful of the guests. They're your first, your last, your everything.

objects in our daily lives, our life itself becomes a sort of training. We come to use each tool with deep care and consideration as we do in tea. Then, the way a person lives makes tradition."

Wabigokoro asks us to pay close attention to nature's cycles of growth, decay, and rebirth, to follow the rhythm of the seasons as they ebb and flow. We all know that without winter's dim afternoons we couldn't have summer's brilliant evenings. Sometimes, though, as the days grow smaller and a sad but certain sense of rest envelops the earth, it's hard not to wish summer could last forever. The oaks and maples shed their leaves and give their mighty souls a respite from production. Yet deep into midwinter, we humans continue to churn through our daily routines, asking ourselves to muster up the same vigor we had during the long days of June.

The practice of using subtle symbolic messages to suggest the seasons is a key part of tea, known as *toriawase*. When I went to

The earth is designed with four seasons— at least in the higher latitudes—one of birth, one of florescence, one of harvest, one of contemplation. Despite war, and acts of ruthlessness, Nature preserves her subtle intent.

—POET SPARROW,
IN *THE SUN*,
DECEMBER 2001

tea in Tokyo in early June, I was served a beautiful sky blue sweet (*omogashi*) with four sections, evoking the hydrangeas that were blooming all across the countryside. A single peony, still wrapped into itself in a tight ball, graced the alcove (*tokonoma*), the spot reserved for a seasonal scroll of Zen calligraphy and flowers. Tea was served in a wide, shallow bowl, in accordance with Rikyu's rule: "In the summer try to bring out the feeling of coolness, in the winter the feeling of warmth." Had it been January, we would have drunk from tall, narrow bowls that allowed the tea's vapor to wash over and warm our faces, and our sweets would have been steamed.

In our own daily lives, practicing wabi-sabi means welcoming each seasonal turn and the changes it brings to our surroundings as well as our psyches. This can mean allowing yourself to let go of a few extracurriculars to make room for a midwinter nap. It can be as easy as arranging a vase full of tulips in April or frost-kissed raspberry branches in October. You can taste the seasons in the food you choose: early spring greens, summer's sweet berries, fall's savory squashes, winter's slightly bitter root vegetables. (I happen to think turnips, with their bitter, earthy acquired taste, are among the most wabi-sabi of foods.) Resisting year-round asparagus and tomatoes is the mark of a wabi-sabi warrior.

While I was in Japan, I went to a French restaurant in Kasama City, a small pottery center outside of Tokyo, with three Japanese friends. When we ordered, the waiter asked if we would prefer rice or bread. "Well, bread, of course," I answered, smug in my assumption that this was the right choice with French fare.

"I am sorry," said my friend. "I am Japanese." He ordered a bowl of rice for himself, and chopsticks with which to eat it.

Our French meal was served on local pottery, the soup barely covering the bottom of tall earthenware bowls, the fish on rough square platters. I buttered my bread with a silver knife, and my friend lifted his bowl to scoop rice into his mouth. Was the pottery

## NATURAL ORDER

Two hundred years ago, a wealthy patron commissioned Japanese Zen monk and artist Sengai to produce a work of calligraphy. Sengai wrote, "A parent dies, a child dies, then a grandchild dies."

The patron was furious that he'd been offered this simplistic and obvious message, but Sengai gently rebuffed his complaints. "There can be no greater happiness," he said, "than to live a life that follows the natural order of things."

too primitive to complement the French cuisine? Was the French cuisine even French? No one really cared. The fish was delicate and sweet, and each course was more beautiful than the last. The company was good, and the moment was as authentic as we could have wanted it to be.

In discussing wabi-sabi, this loaded word *authentic* pops up again and again. But what exactly does that mean? Who's to judge whether something is authentic or not? Should anyone be allowed to define it for someone else? My answer is no. Only you can decide what is truly authentic to you.

# zen

## THE SEVEN PRINCIPLES OF ZEN

Zen's seven ruling principles are guiding lights in the wabi-sabi aesthetic.

**✳ FUKINSEI (asymmetry)** Stiff, formal symmetry, suggesting frozen finality and artificial perfection, can be fatal to the imagination. Asymmetry lets us be loose and spontaneous—more human than godlike. It means we can get by with one—or three—candlesticks, and all the china doesn't have to match.

**KANSO (simplicity)** Zen eschews gaudy, ornate, and overembellished in favor of sparse, fresh, and neat. It's the triumph of craftsman style over the cluttered Victorian parlor.

**KOKO (austerity)** Zen asks us to reduce everything to "the pith of essence." Don't love it? Can't find a use for it? Let it go.

**✳ SHIZEN (naturalness)** Zen is artless, without pretense or self-consciousness. It's bare wood, unpolished stone, and flowers from the backyard.

**YUGEN (subtle profundity)** Within Zen lies a deep reserve, a mysterious, shadowy darkness. The hint of soft moonlight through a skylight would be *yugen*.

**✳ DATSUZOKU (freedom from worldly attachments)** The Buddha taught us not to be bound to life, things, or rules. "It is not a strong bond, say the wise, that is made of iron, wood, or hemp," he said. "Far greater an attachment than that is the longing for jewels and ornaments, children and wives." It's the simplicity movement, not keeping up with the Joneses.

**SEIJAKU (silence)** Inwardly oriented, Zen embraces the quiet calm of dawn, dusk, late autumn, and early spring.

I was once the editor of a high-end design magazine featuring second and third homes, usually decorated by professionals. Many homes I visited were lovely, exquisitely appointed—some with wabi-sabi-ish items such as primitive wooden troughs and antique Mexican doors—and, so often, dead. These houses were showcases for the designers, and they lacked any hint of the residents' hearts and souls. It's no wonder these homeowners spent barely two or three weeks each year there. Their homes had nothing to do with who they really were.

In our homes, practicing authenticity means letting go of compromise—and each of us has a different degree of tolerance and trust in ourselves. I couldn't stand the thought of ordering my dining-room chairs from a catalog or picking them up at a chain store, so I lived with hand-me-downs from my parents until I found midcentury Knoll chairs that I love (and could afford). I use those chairs at least three times a day, and they give me no small amount of satisfaction. I'm glad I waited.

I never want to feel like I should make excuses or apologize for anything in my home. ("Well, I really don't like this bedspread, but it was on sale and I was tired of shopping.") If my home is indeed a sanctuary, I want to treat everything I bring into it as sacred. That may mean living without for a while, which is hard for me. Yet every time I've decided I could make do with a household item because I was tired of waiting for the right one to show up, I've regretted it. I despise the vinyl my husband and I chose for our kitchen floor in a moment of desperation at the end of our house renovation, when funds—and patience—were running low. Now

A person who has not found one's essential self cannot grasp the true meaning of wabi.

—TEA MASTER JO-O

37

I'm stuck with it. I can't bring myself to dump perfectly good flooring into the landfill—and it *is* perfectly good, if ugly and plastic, definitely not something that fits into my wabi-sabi vision. I just have to look at it as a daily reminder of what happens when I choose expediency over authenticity.

Coming to terms with this authenticity—what is true to you—is first a process of discovering and embracing your own taste. That changes over time, of course, and you must be willing to discard what you've grown out of. Again, this isn't easy. Lately I've been decluttering—again—and I've struggled to let go of the rusty iron candlesticks that just can't find a home. I still really like them—they're very wabi-sabi in nature—but they're too cumbersome to fit comfortably in my little house. So they're retired from service, at least temporarily. I suspect that if and when I do bring them out again, it will be because I've found the right place for them, and I'll love them all the more.

Six easy steps to awakening your wabi-sabi mind

**GIVE YOURSELF FIVE MINUTES OF QUIET** time each day. If you like it, work up to twenty. Slowly.

**VISIT A FLEA MARKET** or junk shop. Don't buy anything. Just walk around and note what really appeals to you. Okay, if you see something you *must* have, go ahead and take it home.

**TAKE A DAILY OR WEEKLY WALK OUTDOORS.** Keep a mental or written log of seasonal changes (color, light, and nature's mood) that you observe.

**MAKE SOMETHING—ANYTHING:** a painting, a piece of pottery, a driftwood picture frame. Place it in your home where you'll see it often. Admire it. No matter what it looks like.

**PLACE ONE FLOWER, BRANCH, OR STEM** you've found outside your door in a place where you'll see it every day: your desk, your bedside table, next to the refrigerator. When it catches your eye, stop for a second or two and admire its singular beauty.

**CREATE A TREASURE ALCOVE.** Place something you value (anything you want, from an heirloom to a stone) in a special place. Replace it every season, then every month, and eventually every day.

# give space a chance

# feel

It's been said that modern Americans face more choices in one trip to the grocery store than our grandparents faced in their entire lifetimes. All that freedom of choice is certainly reflected in most of our homes, littered with more furnishings and gadgets than we will ever really need. Our attachment to all this stuff is a major impediment to becoming a wabibito. Learning to let go of our media-driven desires for more, more, more and instead creating space in which to cultivate serenity is the first step toward a wabi-sabi home.

It's not the tragedies that kill us, it's the messes.

—DOROTHY PARKER

Take a good look around your house. Chances are, you'll discover an awful lot of visual noise. Do you really need a TV in every room, a collection of glass ducks, and all those sweaters that no longer fit (but might again some day)? Does your daughter really need all those wild-haired, legless Barbies languishing in their own messy Barbie houses? You probably know, deep down, that the clutter you've parked in your home over the years is as destructive to your well-being as the constant buzz of a nearby highway . . . and the thought of actually doing something about it is absolutely paralyzing.

Wabi-sabi gasps for breath in a home littered with stuff. If the basis of wabi-sabi is emptiness and space, homes rife with gadgets (even if all of them work) and tchotchkes (even if all of them are beautiful) will never be able to deliver the wabi-sabi promise of serenity. Clutter brings dust that smudges our clarity, both physically and metaphorically. It gets in our way.

If wabi-sabi is all about letting go of attachment to the material world, it drowns in the sea of things you have to hold on to because they were expensive, because they were gifts from your mother-in-law, because you just might need them some day. Wabi-sabi thrives in a home where space and light are allowed to prove their merit as the most desirable ornament. As designer Philippe Starck has pointed out, we're always at our most creative and productive when we're living very simply.

But we Westerners struggle mightily with all of our possessions. Every year, several books full of advice on uncluttering and organizing are published; most daily newspapers revisit the subject regularly. Those newspapers are part of the problem; every day, the

42

average household accumulates 300 pages of paper (240 of them never used). According to the Self Storage Association, the average person accommodates four and a half tons of material goods, including clothing, accessories, appliances, and furniture. Experts say that most of us have 25 percent more furniture and 75 percent more toys than we need. Professional organizer Julie Morgenstern asserts that we actually use about 20 percent of the stuff we own; the rest is simply clutter. "Tangible clutter is anything that creates stress because of its appearance, condition, location, arrangement, and/or quantity," states organizing expert Harriet Schechter. "Having too much of a good thing can create just as much clutter as keeping lots of not-so-good things."

A couple of years ago I gave a workshop called "Making Your Home Your Sanctuary" in New York City. Before we got under way, each of us talked about what we loved—and hated—about our homes. Almost every single participant mentioned clutter as his or her number one obstacle to a nurturing home. They knew it was there, and they knew it was messing with their serenity. And they felt powerless to do anything about it.

Perhaps New Yorkers, crowded into smaller spaces than most, have a harder time controlling clutter—but I think not. I recently ran into the exact same situation during a photo shoot in rural northern California. Linda, the homeowner, had built herself a stunning straw bale home, meticulously designed to give her abundant space and sunlight. A playwright and artist, Linda had asked her architect to include a large office and studio in the back of the house, but when we scouted it for possible shots, we found we couldn't maneuver through the mess. Linda had set up her computer on an old desk that was falling apart. Shelves were littered with out-of-date phone books and files, and every corner was filled with boxes of assorted stuff. A beautiful heirloom table was shoved into the corner as a place to pile more clutter, and her sculpting table stuck out oddly in the middle of the room. We moved it all out of the way to stage a simple, serene photograph that made the most of the room's sensuous curves. "Oh, my gosh," Linda sighed. "This is actually a really beautiful room. I never come in here, because it's all so overwhelming. I've been wondering how I'll ever finish my next play."

I talked her into dumping the broken desk, and together we moved out all of the files and boxes. Linda pulled the antique table from its corner and set up a work space looking out into the empty room. "There was just too much stuff," she kept saying in amazement. "I've asked so many people how I could make this a nice room, and there was just too much stuff!" As she opened the antique table drawer for the first time since she'd moved in, she was delighted to find a collection of linen napkins she thought she'd lost.

Nothing sells magazines better than cover blurbs promising tips to help readers unclutter. Homes have grown in size over the years to accommodate not more people but greater amounts of stuff. Kids need one helmet for skiing and another for biking, plus scooters and laptops and violins. Parents *need* bread makers and espresso machines and are tempted at every turn by the sheer availability of global goods. Maybe we have so much stuff in our homes because there is simply more stuff available in our world. And as a culture,

44

OPPOSITE:
Built-in storage goes a long way toward eliminating clutter. A child's toys are contained in a basket on the lower-shelf, well within reach.

we haven't been taught to distinguish quality from quantity. In a country where the pursuit of happiness has translated largely into the pursuit of stuff, we panic at the suggestion that clearing some of the clutter might just lead to a more peaceful existence.

"We live in a cluttered world," Dr. Jerrold Pollack, a Portsmouth, New Hampshire, psychologist who studies obsessive-compulsive behavior including excessive shopping, hoarding, and collecting, pointed out in the *Atlanta Journal-Constitution*. "We get more mail, we get more magazines, we have the opportunity to buy more things. One hundred years ago, you couldn't have bought 200 different pairs of shoes if you wanted to. Now you can get that in an afternoon."

So perhaps our cluttered living spaces aren't really our fault. All this great stuff is readily available, and the hunter-gatherer instinct is deeply embedded in our DNA. How can we resist a bread maker that was once $130, now calling to us from the sale table with a markdown sticker of $50? So what if we don't have a place for it; we can always store it in the hall closet until we find one.

"For the overwhelming majority of Americans, an important part of living the good life simply means 'more,'" said trend watcher Daniel Yankelovich way back in 1979, well before the explosion

45

of big-box superstores had begun luring American shoppers with deeply discounted goods. Surrounding ourselves with stuff proves to others that we've made it and fills us with a sense of abundance. "It makes us emotionally comfortable to have things," psychologist Marsha Sauls told the *Journal-Constitution*. "It makes us feel safe."

"Every possession is a symbol of the self," said Georg Simmel in 1910. We show the world—and ourselves—who we are through the goods we amass, the souvenirs of foreign lands, the beacons of our good taste. We assert our fanciful sides by collecting *Wizard of Oz* memorabilia, our intellectual curiosity through shelves upon shelves of books, our unique perspective through the art we choose. "I'd love to just chuck it all and travel around Europe for a year," my friend Rachel said to me the other day. "But what would I do with all my books? There's just no way I can let go of my books."

One in three Americans collects something, a pastime that can easily get out of hand. "It's like alcoholism," admitted Dolph Gotelli, the world's foremost collector of Santa Claus iconography. Deep down, you know that the last thing you need is another toy horse for the dusty collection that's taken over your bedroom. Yet you can't stop looking for them, and you can't help yourself from bringing them home. You've become powerless over your stuff; it has become unmanageable.

An entire profession has grown out of our inability to deal with our own stuff. The National Association of Professional Organizers,

46

Gently, but with undeniable will, divesting myself of the holds that would hold me.

—WALT WHITMAN

based in Norcross, Georgia, embodies a legion of superorganizers who charge anywhere from $25 to $125 an hour to help you get your possessions under control. A brutally honest friend—one who's not afraid to tell you that something is ugly, outdated, or simply too much—is a cheaper alternative.

Last year my friend Hermine, who grew up on a barge in Europe and never had the luxury of becoming a clutterer (she didn't even have a closet), helped me go through my storage spaces one by one. At first it was jarring; those leather coats from the eighties were expensive, and I'd spent $500 on that ugly mirrored chandelier hanging in the garage—it was the first thing I'd bought after my divorce. But after a while the spirit of dispossession began to overtake me. "Ugly!" I'd say gleefully and toss the sweater into the huge Goodwill pile. "Unnecessary!" And away went the spare blender, the one I kept in the laundry room just in case something happened to the one we like to use.

It took an entire summer, but the result was liberating. For the first time in years, I could walk into my storage shed (I literally had to stand outside and toss things in before), and I could find the hedge clippers (we had three pairs, because I could never locate them from one season to the next). We can park the car in the garage—something we hadn't been able to do in years—and my son can play inline hockey in all that empty space. I like every single item of clothing in my closet, and I've made a vow that for everything I bring in, I'll get rid of another. My ultimate goal is to let go of two things for every one I buy, but that's proving to be pretty difficult. I'm just not quite there yet.

47

Uncluttering is nothing more than common sense; there's no magic to it. All the advisories offer the same basic advice, in one form or another. They all go something like this:

- ◥ Don't try to unclutter your entire house at once. Start with a drawer or a shelf and move up to problem areas (like the garage or the basement) once you've had some smaller success.

- ◥ Spend fifteen minutes per day cleaning up the detritus of daily life before it becomes overwhelming.

- ◥ Take everything out of a drawer or closet and spread it out in front of you. You'll eliminate more and organize what's left more efficiently if you can see it all at once. This also gives you a chance to clear out the dust and run a damp rag over the surface.

- ◥ As you clear out, have four boxes or bags marked Keep, Give Away, Throw Away, and Hold for One Year. The last one's for items you don't need or use but just can't bear to part with yet. If you haven't touched them in a year, their time has come.

- ◥ If in doubt, throw it out.

- ◥ If you can't find a good home for something, it's probably time to say farewell.

- ◥ Get rid of two items every time you buy a new one.

✗ ↰ Allow only three items on each surface.

✗ ↰ Cover only about one-tenth of a table with objects of
      differing sizes.

  ↰ Just say no to refrigerator magnets.

✗ ↰ Keep windowsills clear of knickknacks and potted plants.

✗ ↰ Keep clutter contained. Use baskets and bowls to collect
      mail, pens and pencils, loose change, and all the other
      odds and ends that collect on counters and tabletops.

49

The funniest piece of advice I've run into in all the clutter literature I've studied is to keep all the items you don't really want by
your front door and offer them, like parting gifts, to guests as they
leave. In my neighborhood, the tradition is to simply haul whatever
you don't want down to the end of the driveway and put a big Free
sign on it. Someone generally takes it—and we don't have to insult
our friends by offering them our junk. The unwritten law, of course,
is that once you've claimed something, you cannot give it back.

Of course, there's always Goodwill and all the other charitable
organizations that are willing to drive by and pick up your
unwanted items. And in many cities, you can find newsletters,
e-mail listservs, and even physical "swap meet" spaces that accommodate unloading of the stuff you no longer want or need. Once
you've made the decision to divest yourself of clutter, getting rid of
it is the least of your problems. Learning not to replace it with new,
better clutter is the challenge.

## SIMPLE RULES FOR STORAGE

As both the Japanese and Frank Lloyd Wright have taught us, the key to creating serene, uncluttered spaces is having ample storage in which to hide your stuff.

- ❧ Storage areas should account for 10 percent of your home's total square footage.
- ❧ Closets, especially walk-ins, have one-third less storage potential than a storage wall of equal square footage.
- ❧ Flexible storage (movable clothes rods and shelves) allows more efficient use of space.
- ❧ Store items where they're used.
- ❧ Store items at convenient heights—light, small objects higher and heavy, bulky items lower.
- ❧ Store similar items together.

Art is the elimination of the unnecessary.

—PABLO PICASSO

But wait a minute, our inner collector screams. We need our stuff around us; it makes us *us*, it comforts us. Most people aren't comfortable living in the pristine, sterile rooms touted in those monochrome manuals on minimalism. And that's not what wabi-sabi's all about, anyway.

There are definite lines—and they're not even all that fine—between stark, spare, and cluttered. The wabi-sabi room doesn't have to be prisonlike or monkish, completely without ornament or whimsy. It simply asks not to be suffused with extraneous details.

"Our life is frittered away by detail," stated Thoreau, that wabi-sabi hero who, with fellow Transcendentalists such as Ralph Waldo Emerson, believed that living more simply was a means to spiritual clarity. This outlook was heresy in their era, when the amount of furnishings, knickknacks, and heavy brocades crammed into the Victorian parlor signaled wealth and status. "This excess of decoration might be called the 'American disease,'" wrote homekeeping expert Emma Hewitt in 1889. "But let us hope that it has nearly run its course, and that we are learning to have beauty *only* where it is needed and appropriate."

The arts-and-crafts movement, like wabi-sabi in the sixteenth century, emerged as a reaction to the prevailing aesthetic of fussiness and ostentation. "Have nothing in your home that you do not know to be useful or believe to be beautiful," stated William Morris, a founder of the movement, in one of the most often repeated lines in home decorating. Domestic advisers railed unrelentingly against knickknacks and bric-a-brac, advocating unembellished spaciousness and borrowing heavily from Japanese, colonial American, and craftsman traditions.

Not everyone bought that advice: Americans' love affair with Victorian decor was a passionate one. Victorian clutter and arts-and-crafts simplicity managed to live side by side for many years,

51

All of the items on these shelves are lovely, wabi things—there are just too many of them. Eliminating half of the items makes for a more serene, simple look and accentuates the soul of the items that remain. If you can't bear to part with your knicknacks, take a lesson from the Japanese and rotate them in and out of storage according to the seasons.

As this living room proves, minimalism doesn't have to be cold and uninviting. The floors, made from concrete polished like terazzo, are clean yet comfortable, and the built-in window seats provide seating and storage without clutter. The simple palette and restraint in furnishings give this room a serene, cozy ambience.

until Frank Lloyd Wright wedged his ideas about organic architecture deep into the American psyche in the early twentieth century. Rooms should be "backgrounds for the life within their walls," said Wright in explaining the streamlined style, with noticeable lack of decoration and ornament, of his Prairie homes. Just to make sure no one missed this point, he added emphatically, "And no junk!"

As Wright's fame grew in North America, the Bauhaus movement—advocating sleek, technological design and geometric glass—was taking hold in Germany. Closely tied to the international style, a celebration of the technological age in glass, steel, and concrete, these movements were the extreme reaction to Victorian excess. Viennese architect Adolf Loos declared that "ornament is crime," and Swiss-born French architect Le Corbusier asserted that homes should be "machines for living." He shamed the upper classes to his way of thinking by stating, "The more cultivated a person becomes, the more decoration disappears."

Bauhaus and international style prevailed mainly in intellectual circles—not with the general public, the people who were asked to live and work in the cold steel and glass buildings. Yet they paved the way for the stern minimalist movement, a style of conspicuous restraint that emerged in the 1960s.

Minimalist rooms are generally spare on color, furnishings, and any sort of extraneous ornament or decoration. Perfection rules; just the right vase must be placed in just the right spot to inject just the right touch of color into the precisely appointed room. The lines of the furnishings and the room itself must be strong and simple, meticulously designed. Throw pillows, fringe, and family photos are strictly *verboten*. "If you like to collect things and display *objets trouvés* or family heirlooms, then maybe you should get a lock-up garage or a spare room where you can throw things," advised Tyler Brule, former editor of the upper-crust British design magazine *Wallpaper*.

Minimalism has endured and still has fans in design circles. *House and Garden* editor Dominique Browning calls minimalism "a pared-down approach to domestic life that solves the problem of sensory overload," (but admits she's no minimalist herself). Minimalist architect John Pawson, whom *Time* magazine called "the man who made Martha Stewart rethink chintz," claims that the style offers a sense of liberation that's not possible "if one is distracted by the trivial." Pawson's advice to minimalist wannabes is that "every day you have to spend time on deciding what to get rid of." Yet even he had to admit that most of his clients can't resist messing with his austere interiors. "There's no stopping them," he says. "There's always something lying around that alters the focus of the whole room." Like Frank Lloyd Wright, whose response to clients' uncouth tastes was to build in all the furnishings, Pawson designed a collection of sanctioned objects for the clutter-prone that includes a bronze bowl, a white lacquer and cedar tray, and a wooden cylinder candleholder.

Open space, clean lines, and lack of clutter allow light to play brilliantly in this elegant bathroom.

The fact is, many people admire minimalist rooms in photographs and in theory, but most of them don't really want to live in a place where leaving a coffee cup on the side table is considered a mortal sin. Those sleek lines and vast spaces look great, but they're about as warm and inviting as a schoolmarm with a wooden ruler. People with dogs and children can't live in them. "Minimalism requires a discipline that most people don't have," admits architect Deborah Berke, dubbed "Miss Minimalism" by *Wallpaper.* "And it makes anyone who can't resist buying things or doesn't put stuff away or control their children feel lousy about themselves."

In the mid-1950s, *House Beautiful* editor Elizabeth Gordon, never one to mince words or fear the wrath of the design community, railed publicly against the "cult of austerity" that had taken hold of American design. "Today good modern design offers comfort *and* performance *and* beauty," she wrote.

"I cannot help but feel that minimalism offers the enforced calm of the straightjacket, not the sense of ease one would naturally associate with being 'at home,'" designer Terence Conran complains. "If minimalism looks like it's hard work, that's often because it is." Yet Conran also finds nuggets of brilliance in the minimalist room. "It does reveal, like the best of modern architecture, the often unsung beauty of the everyday—the play of natural light, the sheer dynamic of space, and the subtleties of form and texture," he writes in his book *Easy Living.*

In recent years, traditional minimalism has begun to give way to a more wabi-sabi-like minimalism—a kinder, gentler aesthetic that

54

Grace fills empty spaces, but it can only enter where there is a void to receive it.

—SIMONE WEIL

allows for some imperfection, a personal touch or two, and a whisper of whimsy. Even hard-core advocates began to admit that uptight, intellectual minimalism was no fun. Most of them "really have lots of tchotchkes hidden everywhere," architect Gisue Hariri told workshop participants at the Contemporary Furniture Fair in 1997. Brian Carter, the chairman of the University of Michigan's architecture program and a staunch advocate of British minimalism, confessed to the *Minneapolis Star-Tribune*, "I hate to sound like my mother, but it is nerve-racking to imagine trying to vacuum those white walls without scuffing them."

This shift is happening in architecture as well. The work of Tadao Ando is a fine example of today's more human modernism, with a good dose of wabi-sabi thrown in. Heavily influenced by the simple, rustic farmhouses of his native Japan, Ando uses modern materials such as concrete as a means to "carve out spaces that might evoke architecture reduced to the extremes of simplicity and an aesthetic so devoid of actuality and attributes that it approaches theories of *ma,* or nothingness." Ando was first exposed to the work of international style zealot Ludwig Mies van der Rohe when he traveled to the West to study. "In Mies there is something tragic and cruel which wanted to push everything to a totally logical conclusion, completely ignoring all human considerations," he writes. "Mies is dead now, and hopefully the desire to design whatever is most monotonous has come to an end.

"I think modernism and humanism are values which must somehow be able to coexist," Ando concludes, "even if, during our century, they have more often been in conflict." Concurs Thomas

O'Brien, one of today's leading proponents of international style: "In the end, it has to be human."

In our own homes, we must practice a complicated two-step: spacious but not stark, comforting but not cluttered. It's a sensibility best developed and nurtured over time, and it involves refining, then refining again, then refining again. You may live for years with eight candles, a lamp, and a bowl on a side table and then one day realize that removing the candles lets the clean lines of the lamp and the vast possibility of the empty bowl shine through. A hand-knit afghan may be useful on the sofa in winter months, but clutter during the summer.

If you have the luxury, creating spacious rooms is easiest when

starting from scratch. Every room has walls and floors, the surfaces that will provide background to everything else. So start there. You can unify the room and create a sense of serenity and spaciousness by keeping the color scheme simple. You don't have to go for a monochrome look, but you do want the colors to blend easily into one another without sharp contrasts. Light, cool colors such as pale greens and grays will expand the sense of space.

✳ ✳ Keep floor coverings simple—consider solid-color area rugs in natural fibers such as jute or sisal—and do the same for window treatments. Opt for simple shades, venetian blinds, or tab-top panels rather than heavy, layered curtains. On the

✳ ✳ ✳ He who knows he has enough is rich.

—LAO-TZU

walls, one large, simply framed picture is preferable to a grouping.

Now you can start adding elements, one by one. First the largest pieces: sofas, armoires, maybe even the big-screen TV (if it must be there). Try to place these big pieces near the walls rather than out in the middle of the room so they don't act as dividers, carving the space into small parcels. Choose furnishings that sit up off the floors, exposing the floor space underneath. Banish loud, brightly upholstered pieces; keep textures and patterns subtle and simple Choose the kind of pattern that you have to look at closely to discover a pattern at all. Also look for pieces with simple lines and strong, uncomplicated forms: Parsons tables, craftsman-style chairs, American primitive pieces. Eliminate any items—footstools, plant stands, spare chairs—that aren't crucial to the room's comfort. Resist the urge to fill every space in the room.

As you add each furnishing or decoration, stop to weigh its effect on the whole. How does it relate to the others? Are you starting to intrude upon the room's empty, silent spaces? These empty spaces are what Tadao Ando referred to as *ma*, the space between or the balance between objects—and they're crucial. You want your eye to travel without interruption through the room and, ideally, into the next space or outdoors. If your gaze bumps into something along the way, that something needs to be relocated.

The items that remain on this once-cluttered table represent nature, ancestors, and the rustic beauty of traditional crafts. Uncluttering also allows the table itself to shine.

As Frank Lloyd Wright taught us, built-in furniture and shelving go a long way toward creating spaciousness. Also consider furnishings that do double duty as storage, which helps minimize clutter. A wicker chest holding blankets can serve as a coffee table in the TV room; a small chest of drawers makes a great end table. Another advantage to using chests as tables is that it discourages the proliferation of tabletop ornaments. You won't want to move a collection of figurines every time you need a blanket.

Again and again, the advice most often attributed with minimalist living is to eliminate, eliminate, eliminate. You don't have to give away all your family heirlooms or sell the artwork you cherish on eBay. These pieces of ourselves are important, which is why the best example of having it all comes from the ancient Japanese, who understood that just because they owned an item, they didn't *always* have to display it. They rotated artwork through the tokonoma, a special spot for displaying precious items, on a seasonal basis.

The advantages of this are many. It minimizes some of the pain of uncluttering, as you don't have to actually give away the knickknacks that you've accumulated over the years. And it also prevents you from buying much more, as it feels like you're getting something new when you pull things from storage. (But here's the hard part: you have to pledge to rotate something out when this happens!) Think about how much fun it is to unwrap the Christmas tree ornaments and hang them on the tree each year. And think of how ready you are, come January, to put them back into storage. Thinking seasonally, you can expand on this concept throughout the house:

58

replace a heavy woolen comforter with a light linen spring one, store the candles that were so helpful through those long winter nights to make room for spring flowers, display only one piece of the silver tea set at a time. By rotating the accessories in your home, you will not only create new space and light, but you will also come to develop a greater appreciation for your belongings.

## TAKING INVENTORY:
### THREE EASY STEPS TO CLUTTER-FREE LIVING

These guidelines are simple, and they're not new. So, why are they so hard to follow?

**EVERY SIX MONTHS OR SO,** pretend you're moving: Do you really want to haul out six boxes marked "miscellaneous stuff" or ask your friends to carry all those crates of books?

**WEIGH THE VALUE** of each item you own in terms of the effort it takes to clean, maintain, and (perhaps) move. Do you love it so much that it's all worth it? If so, keep it. If not—someone else might.

**BEFORE YOU BUY ANYTHING NEW,** ask yourself whether you can live without it. Walk away from it; if you find yourself pining, go back and get it.

## THE ART OF NOT TOO MUCH

Referred to variously as "the cultivation of the little" or "the cult of the subdued," shibui is the ancient Japanese art of not too much, an economy of means that lends a quiet grace to Japanese homes.

In his book *The Unknown Craftsman*, Soetsu Yanagi points out that Japanese is the only language in which such a word—"a simple adjective to describe a profound, unassuming, quiet feeling"—exists. "Do other peoples possess an equivalent? The lack of the word will mean the lack of the idea and fact," he states. Is it possible for Americans to implement this elusive, Zen-drenched concept, bonded as it is to a faraway culture?

Perhaps. But first we must understand just what this shibui thing is all about.

The ancient Japanese character for shibui had a line that signified a water radical and three of the characters that mean "to stop." The figure referred to the blockage of water—a symbol of restraint.

The Japanese describe shibui as the bitter taste of green tea or the astringent quality of an unripe persimmon. It is tart, not overblown—rough cloth and pottery, not delicate lace and china. A shibui room is subtle, hinting at a deeper, more soulful beauty that must be unearthed. Decorative items are used sparingly, hinting by their very presence that they are more than just pretty things on display. There is refinement, a sense of composure.

The art of shibui doesn't adhere to fashion, trends, or any one particular style. But a few basic tenets do apply. It may help to bear these in mind if you aim to bring this simple beauty into your wabi-sabi home.

- Colors should be subtle and toward the low end of the spectrum: black, gray, slate, dark brown, moss green. Don't use whites, ivories, or loud, showy hues.
- Ornaments should be simple and abstract. Ideally, they should be representative of nature, which signifies the deepest kind of beauty in Japanese culture. Forms should be rounded, with few corners. *Shibuimono*, or shibui things, have a nonmechanistic, timeless beauty: wind-up grandfather clocks, old bottles, worn wooden furniture.
- Wood can be used generously. It should be left unvarnished and untreated but worked over to make the most of its polish, color, and grain.
- Backgrounds and surfaces should be plain and simple.
- Arrangements of flowers or other objects should adhere to the "law" of uneven numbers; three is always ideal. Use as few items as possible.

Chapter 3

you've got the look

# look

Wabi-sabi is understated and imperfect: the much-loved but chipped vase, the old wooden coffee table bearing the scars of toddlers and adults alike, the mystery inherent in a tarnished goblet. This distressed, aged look has burrowed deep into the American appreciation, finding its way into catalogs and shopping malls. But mass-produced faux-old furniture offers only a facade akin to looking at a photograph instead of experiencing the majesty of the Grand Canyon. You can do that, of course, and it might be enough for you. But true wabi-sabi takes time, patience, and a willingness to wait for the perfect antique, heirloom, or flea market find. It means

The voyage of discovery consists not in seeking new landscapes but in having new eyes.
—MARCEL PROUST

learning to trust your instincts and use all of your senses—because creating a "look" is as much about your home's scent, texture, and soul as it is about how it might look on film.

To begin creating a wabi-sabi home, first pay attention to how you look at things. Most of us were taught that perfection is beautiful and anything less—a tablecloth fraying at the corners, a rug faded from brilliant red to pale rose, a coffee table with a deep scratch—should be fixed or replaced with something new and shiny. Our tastes have been honed in a prosperous era; patching and mending are for our Depression-era grandmothers. What we've forgotten, however, is how comfortable and nurturing our grandmothers' homes really were.

Most of our grandmothers understood, inherently, the difference between wabi and slobby. Their tablecloths and linens may have been faded from many washings, but they never had rips or tears in them. Their furnishings had a settled-in quality, but they were never broken down or dilapidated. Their floors showed the wear of many feet, but they were always swept. The rag rugs that warmed those floors weren't fashionable, but they wove together memories in their use of old garments.

That many-dimensional warmth and comfort can't be ordered through a catalog or online. Honing our sense of subtle beauty has nothing to do with our household budget. It's about taking the time to look—really look—at objects. Even before she discovered shibui in the early 1960s, *House Beautiful* editor Elizabeth Gordon wrote, "If you can't find beauty—for free—when you are poor, you won't be likely to have it when you are rich . . . even though you may have bought and paid for it." Gordon urged her readers to look at everything with a "pure eye," letting go of all associations about its price, its age, its social context, and its prestige value. "You have to wipe away all judgments made by others, and merely respond to the object as you do to those things in nature that are moving: trees, sunsets, clouds, mountains," she stated.

As is so often the case with wabi-sabi, the first step in appreciation building is to simply take a walk. Walk slowly, and allow yourself to fully take in the gifts that are available to you. Look at the broad horizons, then narrow your gaze to a pebble. Run your hand over the rough bark of a maple tree, and compare that to the smooth, paper-thin bark of a birch. Check out the many hues and striations in a piece of limestone. Feel how the quality of light changes as a cloud moves over the sun. Taste the melancholy of a late afternoon in November, the exuberance of that same hour in June. But again, put away judgment. It's easy to find beauty in June, with its lush greens and showy purples. Push yourself to feel

OPPOSITE: This rustic table draws its beauty from the natural forms and textures of the branches it's made from.

65

the fragile warmth of the November sun and observe the quiet vulnerability of branches bared to the elements. Consider how garish a blooming rosebush would be against the muddy greens and browns of a November afternoon.

The beauty in November is the assuredness with which it accepts its Novemberness. Pale, low light is kind to dried beige stalks and barren fields. The earth breathes with a sense of quiet, signaling the time is right to go within. After all that manic energy of summertime and harvest, there is relief in the stillness.

Gordon describes this as the "inevitability" inherent in anything beautiful. "Beauty should be quiet enough so you can take it or leave it," she wrote. "It should not jar or distract or be theatrical. It should have enough life so that when you do give it your attention it has profound interest. But it must be quiet enough so you can ignore it."

Adhering to the Japanese principle of *yo-no-bi*, or the beauty of utility, the wabi-sabi aesthete regards function as highly as form. In tea, for example, beauty is said to be seven parts function and three parts aesthetic; objects should look great, be emotionally evocative, and be absolutely functional as well. A vase has simple curves and sensuous glazing, and it also lets you bring fresh flowers into your home. An enamel bowl embodies the sweet, plain design sense of a bygone age and also holds fruit. A chair carries the chisel marks and pegs of long-ago craftsmanship, and it invites you to rest.

66

I find that what your people need is not so much high imaginative art but that which hallows the vessels of everyday use.

—OSCAR WILDE

## THE GIFT OF SEEING

Soetsu Yanagi, the founder of the Folk Craft Museum in Tokyo, was known as the father of the craft movement in mid-twentieth-century Japan and perhaps did more to bring wabi-sabi back into the collective aesthetic sense than anyone else. In *The Unknown Craftsman: Japanese Insight into Beauty*, Yanagi laid out the following guidelines to help people change their way of seeing and understanding beauty—largely by trusting their own intuition.

- Put aside the desire to judge immediately; acquire the habit of just looking.
- Do not treat the object as an object for the intellect but rather as one for the senses alone.
- Just be ready to receive, passively, without interposing yourself. If you can void your mind of all intellectualization, like a clear mirror that simply reflects, all the better.
- This nonconceptualization—the Zen state of *mushin* (no mind)—may seem to represent a negative attitude, but from it springs the true ability to contact things directly and positively.

"When a thing is self-consciously made to be beautiful (as though beauty was the total aim) it never seems to work, and it becomes futile and knickknacky," Gordon wrote. "There has to be some purpose and usefulness about the creating."

For furniture maker Thomas Moser, whose highly sought-after wood furniture is built with simple integrity, this is the bedrock of beauty. "A bird, a butterfly, a spider web—each is constructed of the precise minimum required to do the job well, and not an ounce more," he states. "Function, not superfluous ornament, is the criterion by which nature designs."

W. R. Lethaby, a successor to arts-and-crafts designer William Morris, believed that a work of art is simply "a well-made thing." Shaping a loaf of bread or laying a nice table were art forms, he argued, and modern society was "too concerned with notions of genius and great performers to appreciate common things of life designed and executed by common people." (One of those celebrated geniuses, Leonardo da Vinci, often suggested that his students study the casual weather stains found on walls.) Morris, Lethaby's mentor, encouraged continual meditation on the mundane details of everyday life. And playwright and social critic Oscar Wilde declared in 1882, "For if a man cannot find the noblest motives for his art in such simple daily things as a woman drawing water from the well or a man leaning with his scythe, he will not find them anywhere at all. What you do love are your own men and women, your own flowers and fields, your own hills and mountains, and these are what your art should represent to you."

The Japanese call this hidden beauty in things their "ah-ness." Once you've developed your ability to find this ah-ness in everything around you, you will be well on your way to understanding wabi-sabi.

68

# BASKET CASE

At first glance this basket, just one of dozens of items cluttering the vendor's table at the Tesuque, New Mexico, flea market, was nothing special. It had an ethnic appeal and evidence of some solid handiwork, but it was overshadowed by much more elaborately beaded and bejeweled objects. It was slightly rickety, certainly worse for its long wear.

Yet the basket called to me, and I picked it up for a closer look. It still held a faint smell of smoke in its weave. The leather band around the edges was stolid yet tattered, speaking of much good use. What did this basket hold—fruit, nuts, utensils or tools? The tiny shells were uniform yet irregular, in shades of beige with the palest yellow centers, and they seemed to hold this vessel together. Despite all the obvious knocking about this basket had endured, not one shell was missing.

I was drawn into this basket's history. I imagined its years of service on another continent, wondered about the artisan's refusal to settle for basic utility—the hours spent finding and stringing tiny shells around its perimeter. I carried its loads and sat by its fires. And then I took it home.

Today it holds napkins in my dining room—perhaps not the most noble use it has been put to, but one that brings me a good deal of satisfaction. As I pull the napkins from it to set the table each night, I stop to admire the basket—and all the history it brings to me—and I'm grateful for this tiny connection to another place.

What did this basket hold in its past lives—fruit, nuts, utensils? It brings with it a mysterious past and the marks of a history of good use.

There is a cachet now
in dust. It gives people
a past they haven't had.

—EDITOR MIN HOGG,
WORLD OF INTERIORS

70

Wabi-sabi furnishings and accoutrements may be crude and rustic—often antique—but they are finely, solidly made. They may be so simple that at first you barely notice them, but on second glance you are drawn to examine and admire. Their presence here and now speaks of endurance through generations of use, a whisper of untold stories locked inside.

It takes commitment to search out well-worn pieces that hold real meaning and beauty for you. It would be so much easier to just call an 800 number and order something in exactly the size and color you need. You'll spend hours and hours—many of them fruitless—in flea markets, antique shops, and salvage yards, and the rewards will be slow to come, but palpable. Your home will be unique and soulful, as opposed to safe and hip in shades of beige.

You'll find no small amount of chipped, distressed, and otherwise "shabby chic" furniture in almost every home furnishing store in America these days. It seems everyone's smitten with the wabi-sabi *look*—which is a great entry point into the vast, many-faceted philosophy. Just be mindful when you choose factory-made distress over the scars that come from years of use that you're losing something in translation.

These faux-old pieces just can't satisfy our collective urge to live with a piece of history, perhaps create a heritage we feel we've lost. Many practitioners of Eastern religions, Shintoism in particular, believe that everything—from the human being to the speck of dust—carries a certain vibration. The steady, solid vibrations that come from pieces made slowly and lovingly by hand are often found in antiques, which are defined as anything made before

1830—when the Industrial Revolution was heating up, rapidly replacing craftsmen with machinery.

❦ ❦ ❦   We seek out and hold dear items that resonate with us because they act as symbols of ourselves, according to sociologists Mihaly Csikszentmihalyi and Eugene Rochberg-Halton. In their study *The Meaning of Things: Domestic Symbols of the Self,* the scientists found that most people find more meaning in a battered toy, an old musical instrument, or an heirloom quilt than they do in expensive appliances. They find extensions of themselves in these things, and they actually look to them as reflections of who they are and what they can become.

Finding the truly wabi-sabi takes work—and countless visits to flea markets and antique stores—unless you happen to be one of those fortunate few who find Eames chairs in Dumpsters. (I seem to run into these people all the time when I go on photo shoots for *Natural Home,* and I am always amazed and a bit envious.) For most of us, successful scavenging means digging through piles of musty old junk to find just the right piece and possibly getting out the hammer for repairs (remember that wabi-sabi *doesn't* mean broken down). It also means getting up at the crack of dawn to beat the professionals to the Saturday morning flea markets.

Inspired (at least in name) by Le Marché aux Puces, a Parisian market that sold flea-infested sofas, flea markets have become a huge business—and an important pastime—for Americans. There are more than twenty-five hundred flea markets in the United

Salvage represents an opportunity for creative thinking. These old shoe forms could be used as vases, door stops, or paperweights—just to name a few possibilities.

Rustic, salvaged fixtures
and an antique mirror
give this bathroom a
unique twist.

States, with an average of about two hundred vendors per market. If you're truly serious about collecting, consider a piligrimage to Indiana, where thirteen hundred dealers line interlocking highways along Richmond's Antique Alley, and Centerville (just six miles west) is said to hold more antiques per square capita than any other town in America.

The following are some universal truths that may make your flea-market shopping easier:

- Start with a plan, which will help guide your search. But be ready to scrap it based on what you find.

- Before you go, study a guide to familiarize yourself with market values for the items you're after. (*Kovels'* guides have been around for ages, and now they're online at www.kovels.com.)

- Bring a list of items you want or need, along with specific sizes and room measurements.

- Bring paint samples, fabric swatches, and photos of the rooms you're decorating.

- Bring a tape measure, a notebook, tote bags, and cash.

- Be prepared to haggle—politely, of course. Most antique dealers and flea-market sellers admit that a 20 percent price adjustment isn't all that unusual.

❧ The best selection happens early; the best bargains come at the end of the day.

❧ If you love it, buy it before it's gone—but remember, most purchases are final.

The beauty in flea-market finds is that they don't have to be put to their original use. A lidless teapot can become a flowerpot, an old window a mirror frame. Jelly jars hold pencils and utensils, and old picnic baskets make great side tables that also provide storage. Old shawls and scarves can be draped over stains or other rough spots in sofas.

If you're successful, you'll bring home items that you truly love. Maybe you fell for the robin's-egg blue green of the frying pan or the faded but still flying horse on the corroded oil drum. Maybe the long spout of that rusty old watering can stirred up some memory you'd lost long ago. You might not even be able to explain why you're drawn to some of the things you pick up, but if you follow your heart and bring it home, then the fun really begins.

Also remember, you don't have to be a slave to each item's history. Mix and match Shaker with midcentury modern, American primitive with southwestern. All that really matters it that the items

Keeping a few shawls over the back of the sofa adds handmade character and also provides immediate comfort when the house is chilly. This delicate lily-of-the-valley shawl was hand knit in Estonia; the other is a simple do-it-yourself project.

73

# shibui

## SHIBUI THINGS

In the early 1960s, *House Beautiful* editor Elizabeth Gordon traveled to Japan to learn more about shibui, a concept that she found virtually interchangeable with wabi-sabi. She sent back a list of Western "shibui things" to help Americans comprehend this new idea. Many of these can still be found in antique stores and flea markets. They include:

- Eighteenth-century captain's chests
- Early American cupboards, blanket chests, trestle tables
- Old glass (bubbly, greenish glass of early American Pennsylvania and old Roman oxidized and iridescent glass)
- Certain sparsely patterned pieces of Lowestoft
- Oaxacan black clay jars
- Etruscan black or red Buchero ware
- Shaker furniture
- Danish furniture
- Some eighteenth-century pewter
- Some salt-glaze pottery
- Some Georgian spoons
- Early American dark green glass wine bottles

appeal to you. "The essence of this look is that it's a look for a life-time," says Wendy Lubovich, a consultant for Dayton's Paris Flea Market in Minneapolis. "It's about finding a piece that you love. And you'll find that if you love everything in the room, it will somehow go together."

In your hunt for wabi-sabi furnishings, bear in mind that the items don't have to sport chipping paint, dents, and pockmarks to qualify. Shaker furniture, with its extreme simplicity and reserve, is inherently wabi-sabi. Japanese architect Tadao Ando, one of today's foremost adherents to wabi-sabi, writes that he was completely taken by Shaker furniture during his first visit to the United States. "I was astounded by the freshness of wooden furniture made by the Shakers," he states. "The mood of the pieces was simple and reserved and exerted a restraining and ordering effect on the surroundings. Technically, the furniture was rationally made with no waste of any kind. . . . In the great diversity of modern times, to experience objects representing an extreme simplification of life and form was very refreshing."

Arts-and-crafts pieces, solidly crafted with rough, oversized iron or copper hardware, were in fact inspired by the wabi-sabi aesthetic. Developed in Europe in the 1850s—largely in reaction to the stuffy prissiness of Victorian furnishings and the isolation and repression caused by the Industrial Revolution—arts-and-crafts furnishings heralded a return to simplicity and a rejection of sentimentality. Gustav Stickley brought arts-and-crafts pieces to the American masses at the turn of the century, vowing to "employ

Honesty of materials, solidity of construction, adaptability to place, esthetic effect.

—GUSTAV STICKLEY

75

only those forms and materials which make for simplicity, individuality, and dignity of effect." At the turn of a new century, the style continues to be in vogue, and I suspect the recent surge in all things craftsman signals yet another popular uprising against the alienation of the technological age.

William Morris, the father of the arts-and-crafts movement, promoted the use of natural dyes, hand printing, and simple furniture with spindle backs and rush seats. A diehard socialist, he railed publicly and prolifically against the "swinish luxury of the rich," decorative excess ("gaudy gilt furniture writhing under a sense of its own horror and ugliness"), and the poverty of people who lacked creativity. With a nod to the Shakers, he called for artisans to make furniture "of a refinement making ever so slightly for austerity, and yet full of graceful lines, and curves not so subtle as to exclude all sense of sweetness." He urged builders to use wood but warned that "no artificial method of staining can be anything but a blunder and a shame."

"Everything made by man's hands has a form, which must be beautiful or ugly," Morris said. "Beautiful if it is in accord with nature, and helps her; ugly if it is discordant with nature, and thwarts her; it cannot be different."

The pieces you choose for your wabi-sabi home don't have to be made before that cutoff date of 1830; there is much wabi-sabi in furnishings built from the mid-twentieth century to the present. In the 1960s Danish furniture makers such as Hans Wegner, Borge Mogensen, and Arne Jacobsen put forth crisp, understated designs

The purpose is usefulness, but with a lyric quality—this is the basis of all my designs.

—FURNITURE DESIGNER
GEORGE NAKASHIMA

that seemed to follow in the Shaker tradition. The wooden furniture was allowed to breathe, finished only with a sandpaper rubdown or linseed oil and embellished with natural materials such as leather, cotton, and linen. In America at the same time, Charles and Ray Eames were combining Shaker simplicity and innovation with modern industry, producing furniture of integrity for the masses.

From the 1940s until his death in 1990, George Nakashima became one of the most important furniture designers in America. A quiet artist-craftsman who chose to work in isolation, Nakashima designed a series of furniture for Knoll and an exclusive series for Widdicomb-Mueller. Mass production of Nakashima's designs introduced many Americans to furniture of solid, simple integrity. He outlined his wabi-sabi point of view perhaps most clearly in a 1953 address quoted in the *New York Herald-Tribune:*

> *Fundamentally, I have a primary interest in natural materials: the deep wearing of centuries of weather on the timbers of Horiuji, the clean freshly hand-planed surfaces of Hinoki or Port Oxford cedar, the burls of English oak. I respond to the textures, colors, and the sheer art and craftsmanship of a good fieldstone wall, the stripped beauty of high-strength concrete. The character and history of a wide plank of walnut re-creates the life and death of two hundred years. The story of bitter winters and the searing desert summers of at least a human lifetime shows in the twisted, tortured forms of bitterbrush; the story of a way of life speaks in the beautiful wide unvarnished boards of a tea-house ceiling.*

Inspired by this impressive lineage, Thomas Moser of Maine may be the contemporary artisan who most embodies the wabi-sabi spirit today. Moser's cherry furniture is classic and enduring, eschewing stains, lacquer, and other veneers, which he believes are usually ways of concealing inferior design, workmanship, or materials of dubious qualities. "The perfect piece of furniture, to me, is one that respects the materials from which it is made, fits the human body, and is comfortable, durable, and archetypal, giving the impression that adding, subtracting, or changing the proportions of any element would make it worse," states Moser, in what could be a modern wabi-sabi treatise.

78

George Nakashima's simple, graphic console has become a classic.

At first glance, designers Charles and Ray Eames don't present themselves as wabi-sabi heroes. The husband-and-wife team worked hand in hand with corporate postwar America, and they loved to play around with new industrial materials such as molded plywood and plastic. Yet in their own way, they adhered to the wabi-sabi philosophy, bringing ideas of democracy in design and access to the masses, using minimal materials, and producing items for everyday use that were both beautiful and affordable. Their enduring furniture designs were a breath of fresh air for many Americans in the midcentury (and beyond), who wanted a contemporary look but found extreme modernism cold and sterile. They produced modernist pieces that designer Sir Terence Conran calls "intensely human, charming, and kind."

The Eameses were probably best known for their ubiquitous molded plywood chair, which has been produced since 1946 by Herman Miller. Perhaps a better example of their wabi-sabi appeal, however, is the 1956 plywood-and-leather "potato chip" lounge chair, which has been described as having "the warm, receptive look of a well-used first baseman's mitt." This piece embodies their simple, artfully restrained, yet delightful style. According to Charles, it has "a sort of ugliness to it."

"It is alive," designer Tibor Kalman wrote of the lounge chair in 1996. "It can be lived with, seen every day, change and evolve, and slowly reveal its beauty. Like a lover. And it's a chair."

Craig Hodgetts, the designer of a recent Los Angeles exhibition on Charles and Ray Eames, points out that what the designers left out of their designs—"the pomposity, hierarchy, and stodginess associated with 'important' stuff'"—is just as crucial as what they put into them.

The Eameses often stated that their goal was to help people see beauty in everyday objects. Charles Eames's grandson, Eames Demetrios, recalls that as a child he spent hours following his grandfather around as he took pictures of cobwebs. Charles didn't believe in pushing kids to hone their art appreciation in museums or galleries; he preferred spiders and picnics. "Make them enjoy the ephemeral," he stated. "Let them learn to express an everyday thing in a beautiful way."

Perhaps the Eameses' wabi-sabi aesthetic was most evident in their infamous Pacific Palisades home, one of the Case Study houses built in the late 1940s. Sponsored by *Art & Architecture* magazine, the Case Study program promoted houses that would accommodate a more casual, modern lifestyle following World War II—and the Eames house did not disappoint. Built with the same eye for simple, clean lines as their furniture, the Eames open-plan home was modern yet human, with a decidedly Japanese influence that included vertical-louvered blinds, tatami mats, and Isamu Noguchi paper lanterns. It demonstrated to many people the freedom that could be found in straightforward, unpretentious design.

The Eames home had a humble, fleeting quality, perhaps best described in a brief that they wrote in 1945, calling for "a large, unbroken area for pure enjoyment as space in which objects can be placed and taken away . . . driftwood, sculpture, mobiles, plants, constructions, etc." Their living room was home to a continually changing collage of Indian embroideries, Mexican clay dolls, ceramic bowls, antique toys (which they collected as fine examples of design principles), and dried desert weeds—all of which existed happily alongside pieces of their mass-produced furniture.

The Eames home, like their furniture designs, is a wonderful example of how lighthearted wabi-sabi can be. Shedding the heavy presence of pretentious high design leaves more space to simply enjoy the rudiments of everyday life—to spend long afternoons photographing cobwebs. Rolf Fehlbaum, a longtime friend of the Eameses, said the couple took such enjoyment from daily life that they never took holidays. "They didn't need them," he says, "they enjoyed themselves so much."

Pollution is nothing but
the resources we are
not harvesting.

—BUCKMINSTER FULLER

Over the past decade materials salvaged from abandoned or demol-
ished buildings—shutters, windows, columns, bricks, fixtures—
have become a design staple. Homeowners and designers with
wabi-sabi leanings have snapped up centuries-old iron gates to use
as wall hangings, turned mantels into headboards, and divided
rooms using old shutters. Solid, handcrafted beams made from
woods that are no longer available add permanence and long-lost
quality to new homes.

82

The use of salvaged materials is a positive trend is many ways.
Environmentally, it's a boon, keeping debris out of landfills and
mitigating the use of new resources. For homeowners, salvaged

Salvaged home
accents and building
materials, such as this
milk-glass lamp and
weathered barn door,
bring depth and soul
into your home.

A hundred years ago, old-growth hardwoods were abundant in America, used to build everything from warehouses to homes. But our love affair with these trees, some of which took centuries to mature, eventually led to the decimation of America's old-growth forests. Today, the best way to get quality, old-growth wood is to buy vintage boards that have been salvaged from barns and abandoned warehouses or reclaimed logs that dropped off of barges as they were sent downstream.

"Perfectly imperfect" is how Sandy Conklin of Conklin's Authentic Antique Barnwood and Hand Hewn Beams describes salvaged wood. Full of knots, nail holes, and cracks, this wood also offers density, tight grain patterns, and deep color that simply can't be found in today's wood. Unlike trees harvested today, the old trees had more dense durable heartwood than softer sapwood.

**RED OAK:** Once used as barn siding, and flooring, this strong, heavy wood has a straight grain and pinkish red heartwood.

**WHITE OAK:** Once used in post-and-beam construction, factory roofs, barn siding, and flooring, this yellow-colored wood is durable and rot resistant.

**TULIP POPLAR:** Once used for log cabins, this yellowish, uniformly textured wood is easy to work with.

**CHESTNUT:** Once used in post-and-beam construction, planking, flooring, and siding, this golden to reddish wood is now rare and very desirable.

materials bring charm and interest—and often provide a link to the community. When I visit homes for the magazine, homeowners love to tell me that their wide-plank heart pine floor came from a schoolhouse just down the road or that the cabinets in the kitchen were once in the local university's chemistry building. If it's feasible, bringing home architectural items from your travels and implementing them into your home is a much better reminder of your journeys than a souvenir trinket. One of my favorite homes in Austin derives much of its charm from the Moroccan and Indian architectural tidbits picked up by the homeowner, who had lived in many faraway lands.

Building materials can be found in salvage yards, at garage sales and flea markets, through classified ads, and increasingly through online resources. While the Internet offers a convenient means of searching, it's probably not the most wabi-sabi method. As with flea market finds, salvage should be studied and touched to determine whether there's chemistry before you bring it home to live with. As anyone who's ever booked a date or a hotel room online knows, digital photos can be very deceiving.

Be prepared to dig through piles of musty windows and rusty fixtures before you find what you're looking for. Salvage yards often—but not always—group items by category, but the user-friendliness ends there. Salvaging is a scavenger's game, and you can expect to get dirty. Be on the lookout for rusty nails and tin, and make sure your tetanus shot is up to date. Always check for loose nails before grabbing hold of old wood, and be aware that the paint clinging to that wood might contain lead. If that's the case,

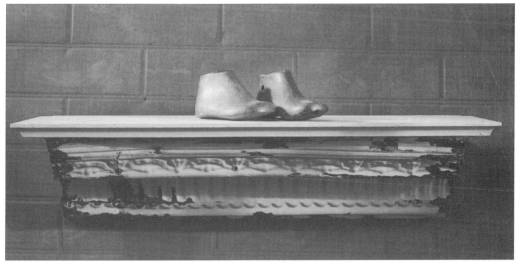

don't strip it yourself; seal it with clear polyurethane (to keep the distressed look) or to have a professional paint over it.

You also want to check all items carefully to make sure they're not too rotten to resurrect. Attempting to salvage the unsalvageable will lead only to frustration and waste your time. Check shutters for loose corner joints and broken slats. A few of these may be acceptable if you don't need functional shutters, but too many will end up looking dilapidated. Check stone items for cracks and stains; these are almost impossible to fix. When salvaging bricks, try to find out when they were fired. Production controls were tightened in the 1940s; bricks made before then aren't as durable.

Again, the fun of salvage is figuring out what to do with it. You can always use the material in its rightful form—beams and doors are eminently reusable. Or you can give it new live in a reincar-

You can make pieces of molding and lintels more functional by adding a top and turning them into shelves. The beauty of this molding, salvaged from a Victorian home, is allowed to come through because the shelf is not cluttered with too many items.

nated form. Corbels make great shelf brackets. Columns (particularly plain Doric columns—the most wabi-sabi type) can be turned into table bases. Windows can be fitted with mirrors, and shutters can become headboards.

Will salvage save you money? Not likely. As the popularity of salvage has surged, the price of many items has become pretty dear. Salvaged flooring (recovered from old buildings and from logs lost at the bottom of rivers in the late nineteenth century) can cost almost double what new flooring costs. But bear in mind that you're getting much higher quality old-growth wood—from trees up to four hundred years old—and that for every two thousand square feet you use, you're sparing an acre of woodland. And while bargains are still out there—especially in places like Habitat for Humanity resale stores—be aware that if you can't install it yourself, you're in for a hefty handyman bill. A couple of years ago I was thrilled to find old french doors for $70 at my local recycled building materials center. They were shorter than current code, though, and it cost me $1,200 to have a carpenter refit the doorjamb so we could use them. I still think it was worth it. The doors add quirky charm to our dining area that standard off-the-rack ones just couldn't match.

86

ABOVE: The door to this bathroom was salvaged from the women's room of an old bank. The wood used around the basin is from a locust tree that was in the homeowners' backyard. OPPOSITE: While you may not want to use rusty hinges for their original purpose, you could find all sorts of other uses for them. They make great wall hooks, for example.

Color, especially in home decorating, can be overwhelming and, yes, even scary. We're seduced by delicious, provocative paint chips: Crème Caramel, Sunset Journey, Misty Dewdrop. We spend tortured hours hanging the little squares on our walls, painting test swaths, checking them from all angles. And still, when all four walls are bathed in Cool Cucumber, we wonder if it's not the same pukey green as the halls of our elementary school. There's a certain safety in white.

But wabi-sabi is never white—it's not even beige. It borrows from the autumnal landscape—hues ranging from soft slate gray to matte gold, with occasional spots of rust breaking the subtle spectrum. It's sinewy, flecked browns and yellowed greens, the myriad shades of stone and moss.

In the absence of spring and summer's brilliant color palette, the eye works harder—and that hard work is rewarded. Finding color inspiration in autumn fields is more challenging than claiming the sunny yellows of spring daffodils, but the result is ultimately more serene and sophisticated. "Be restrained rather than overluxurious in color, or you weary the eye," advised William Morris, who borrowed much of his wisdom straight from the Japanese. And indeed, Japanese tradition holds that bright colors tire the eye—which then tires the body and the soul. The quiet softness of green grays and gray blues has the opposite effect, inspiring peace.

The Babel of modern color, which artists can regard less as a miracle of science than as a phenomenon of culture, is something that many artists have wanted to keep at arm's length.

—ART CRITIC JED PERL

87

88

This early twentieth-
century iron chair once
graced a New York
sanitarium. The wall
behind it is textured with
an easy-to-use natural
clay plaster that brings
more depth and closer-
to-nature color than
chemical-based paint.

The key is to pay close attention to how nature works with color. Forget about the Crayola approach of straight green grass and true blue sky; nature never works in just one shade. The underside of silvery clouds is lilac. From far away, a stone may look like a big slab of menacing gray. Get closer. It's speckled with graduating shades, from deep and dark to nearly white and crystalline, with tidbits of orange and red. Small swatches of the most vibrant colors wash into the larger scheme of quiet, recessive color. It's as if they're there simply to balance the browns and grays and keep it all from getting monotonous—and it works.

The wabi-sabi palette also derives from the natural effects of weather and age, which create irregularity and distortion in color. The sun burns deep striations; the wind mottles; the rain rusts. The wear and tear of an old barn engages us, invites us to look again at the dank red melding into warm brown melding into battered gray. An old car rusts gracefully in a field, transforming from an eyesore into a natural part of the colorscape.

To brush your home with wabi-sabi color, first take a walk (preferably in late fall or winter). Note the color combinations, how they graduate into one another, the ratio of strong color to paler, more washed hues. Translate the overall outdoor color scheme indoors with a paint job in the most dominant colors, draperies and furnishings in subtle variations, and throw pillows as the punctuating bright spots. You might even bring those annoying little color squares from the paint store with you during your exploring; plunk one down and ask yourself if Desert Sage really makes the grade against the real thing.

Better yet, choose naturally pigmented paints over chemically induced colors. Because they're derived from plants, natural pigments are more subtle—and you don't have to work as hard to mimic what's outside the door. A great way to add texture as well as subtle natural color is to mix dried strawflowers, straw, wheat, or even mica chips into a final coat of plaster before applying it. This provides the kind of color you want to touch as well as look closer into—truly wabi-sabi.

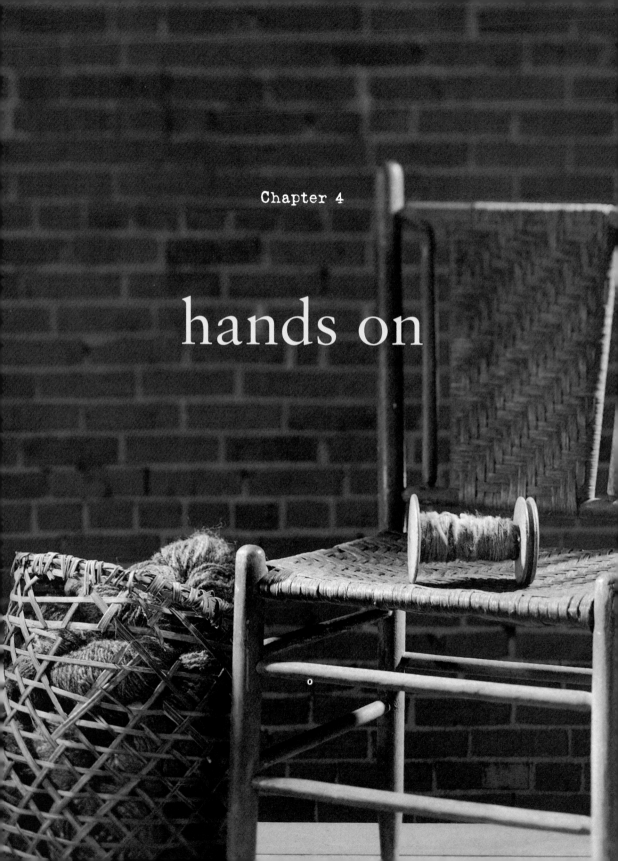

Chapter 4

hands on

# create

What's with this knitting thing? Everyone seems to be doing it. Urbanites from New York to Los Angeles are forming knitting circles and even have their own institution: the Church of Craft. The number of new web sites and magazines devoted to making things by hand grows by day. Trendicators are calling knitting "the Nintendo of the twenty-first century," and according to the Craft Yarn Council of America, a new recruit joins the thirty-eight million other knitters in America every minute.

I wanted to be one of them. Lured by the luscious and expensive skeins of mohair and lambswool at my local knitting shop and encouraged by my office

Handmade things with all their wonderful, charming imperfections have a very rare value. Any craft as applicable and pragmatic as knitting has a great future.

—TREND PREDICTOR
FAITH POPCORN

mates—all of whom were whipping out hats and sweaters at lunchtime and during Stitch 'n' Bitch parties that sounded like a lot of fun—I took up the needles. It seemed a wabi-sabi thing to do— I could relax, make my own dishcloths, revolt against the techno-machine. I never quite got the knack of casting on, but with the help of my colleagues, I managed to produce a scarf for nearly everyone I knew.

I liked knitting. It gave me something to do during my son's hockey practice. I was ridiculously proud of my scarves—even their many mistakes and imperfections seemed charmingly wabi-sabi. I guess I fell victim to the knitting phenomenon that M. Joan Davis, a retired philosophy professor and knitting teacher, describes as the lure of total control. "So many things in life you can't have to yourself, you can't have total control," she says. "With knitting, you can—you pick the colors, the pattern. Every stitch is yours."

And then, just like that, my knitting obsession ended. I didn't know anyone else who needed a scarf, and I dreaded moving on to socks or afghans, which would require patterns and counting and probably even learning how to purl. I was totally intimidated by the web site www.learntoknit.com. I stashed the needles and the yarn remnants on a shelf in my laundry room and didn't give them another thought until it came time to write this chapter—all about the importance of making things yourself in a world of mass production and learning to quiet your mind and your home in the spirit of wabi-sabi.

My life is worthwhile
even if I burn all the
cookies. The creative
process for me is like a
path of discovery, so
mostly my emotions
through it are wonder
and curiosity.

—CHURCH OF CRAFT
COFOUNDER
CALLIE JANOFF

The arts of spinning wool, making pottery, and weaving baskets yield more than just wabi-sabi items for your house They provide a tactile meditation almost impossible to find anywhere else.
My friend Katrina tells me nothing calms her more than sitting
down at her loom—it can cure her of the worst cases of jitters or
blues, she says. She's also the one who taught me about "coping
knitting" before I embarked on a stressful business trip. "Coping
knitting" is a means of tuning out stress-inducing events—and even
personalities—by focusing all your attention on your needles. I
know men and women who excel at handcrafts, and I do think
they're calmer and more centered than I am. Herbert Benson, pres-
ident of the Mind/Body Medical Institute at Harvard Medical
School, backs me up on this, asserting that "any activity, including
knitting, that involves repetition of a word, sound, prayer, phrase,
or muscular activity, coupled with the disregard of everyday
thoughts, elicits the relaxation response."

During my knitting stint, I did feel calmer as I set stitch upon
stitch, slowly building something that no machine could make better. You just can't buy the satisfaction of making something yourself. Yet I'd put away my knitting, and I never did learn to spin, or
weave, or throw pots, despite many good intentions. As a working
mother, I just never had the luxury.

I invited my boss, Linda Ligon, who knits and weaves and
spins—and owns several magazines devoted to fiber arts—to
lunch. "What am I going to do?" I wailed. "I'm not crafty. I don't
know anything about the domestic arts. I'm a fraud."

93

## BREAK IT, MAKE IT

Decorating with broken mosaic tile brings wabi-sabi satisfaction in many ways. It's an easy way to create something yourself—no precision is required. This sunroom floor was made using salvaged tiles—most tile stores are happy to give away boxes of tiles that have broken in transit— and remnants.

In my mind, nothing's easier—or more wabi-sabi—than broken mosaic tiling. You get to make use of old, damaged tiles that might otherwise clutter up a landfill. I have a shed full of overruns from a decorator friend and broken tiles from stores where the owners are happy to give them away for free. You can also implement broken glass and dishes, pottery shards, and other odds and ends such as fossils and stones into your designs. Also consider cementing in personal artifacts such as coins minted in your children's birth years.

There's nothing exacting or precise about broken tile mosaics; imperfection rules. Making mosaics is a thoughtful, meditative process that allows you to turn whatever materials you have at hand into something greater than the sum of its parts. Hone your tiling skills with simple projects such as flowerpots and mirror frames before moving on to more permanent surfaces such as countertops and floors.

**START WITH A CLEAN, DRY SURFACE.** For countertops or floors, it's best to glue tile to concrete or a cementitious surface such as wonderboard.

**YOU CAN DRAW A DIAGRAM FOR YOUR DESIGN** (on paper or directly onto the surface), or you can let it emerge as you tile.

**COLLECT THE TILES YOU PLAN TO USE.** Wrap a tile in an old towel, put on safety glasses, and break the tile with a hammer. The pieces can be as small or as large as you want them to be.

Separating large pieces from small can be helpful; also make a separate pile for tiny shard-like pieces that are useful for filling in gaps.

**USING A TROWEL WITH TEETH**, spread a thin layer of mastic (available at home supply centers in powder that you mix with water or in premixed form) on an area of the surface large enough to let you lay down about a dozen tiles at a time before it dries. The exact size of this area depends on the amount of humidity in your climate and how quickly you can lay tile. Because I tend to deliberate about each piece, I sometimes use a butter knife to spread mastic on each tile individually, then lay it down on the clean surface.

**FIRMLY PLACE TILE** on top of mastic. Continue to spread mastic and place tile until design is complete.

**LET MASTIC DRY** for at least twenty-four hours (more if you live in a damp climate), following manufacturer's directions.

**MIX POWDERED GROUT WITH WATER** according to manufacturer's directions. Wearing rubber gloves, spread the grout over a section of tile with your hands, using your fingers to fill all cracks and crevices.

**USING A SPONGE AND CLEAN WATER**, wipe excess grout off tiles. Continue to rinse and wipe until tile is clean.

**LET GROUT DRY** according to manufacturer's directions.

As she so often does, Linda set me straight. "I've been to your house," she said. "You may not spin or weave, but you've created an incredible feeling there. Everything in it was chosen with care. You've built a lovely garden. You've served me thoughtful meals. And what about your tile work?"

Some years ago, my friend Carlos Alves taught me how to make mosaics with broken tiles, and I've always loved it because—as he promised—anyone can do it. It requires no precision. You can make the broken tile pieces as big or as small as you like, and the spaces between them don't have to be uniform. I started out making flowerpots and tables, and I've since tiled my sunroom floor, both bathrooms, and my kitchen counters and backsplash. Just like knitting, tiling is meditative and satisfying. One piece leads to another leads to another, and then you get to step back and admire how far you've come.

Maybe tiling came so easily to me because Carlos just wouldn't let me be afraid of it. The funny thing is, people look at my floor or my backsplash, and they assume I have some sort of talent that they don't. They try to hire me to do their floors. I explain that it's simply a matter of breaking tile, slapping it down, and grouting it—truly, anyone can do it. And I guess that's exactly what the knitters in my office are trying to tell me about making socks.

A lot of us, it seems, just aren't programmed to believe in our own abilities. We think we can't provide ourselves with the things we need—so we run to the store and buy them. We tell ourselves we don't have the time, talent, or tenacity to braid our own rugs or knit

96

Fortunately, people are artists who know it not—bootmakers (the few left), gardeners and basketmakers, and all players of games. We do not allow shoddy in cricket or football, but reserve it for serious things like houses and books, furniture and funerals.

—W. R. LETHABY

ourselves sweaters. Or maybe more than anything, we just lack the desire. Why bother, when our household needs can be had—cheaply and conveniently—at the nearest superstore?

There are all sorts of reasons to bother, of course—from the poltical (exploitation of sweatshop labor) to the practical (a lot of the stuff we buy these days just isn't well made). But the most important reason is our own personal fulfillment. Creating an intricately patterned tile floor in my sunroom was backbreaking, tedious work that required the help of many friends. Now that floor holds memories of the sweltering weekends we spent tiling and talking late into the night. It's also more elaborate and much more interesting than any professional installation I could have afforded. I'm proud of that floor—and it helped me create a more solid bond with my home. Once it was complete—which took nearly a year of on-and-off weekends—I vowed never to move.

I experienced the ineffable satisfaction of craft. My boss, Linda, points out that there's a huge difference between the satisfaction she gets from weaving a long, simple warp and the drudgery of stuffing envelopes (which she spent a summer doing as a kid). Both require long periods of repetitive, monotonous movement. The difference, she says, is that when she's weaving or knitting, she's driven toward creating a permanent, unique product—a piece of immortality that transcends the finite particulars of her life.

We no longer have to make what we need for daily living, but for many the desire lingers—and even surges as a strong cultural movement from time to time (witness the current generation of hip knitters). Throughout history—from the Mayans to the medieval-

97

ists to the primitivists of seventeenth-century New Mexico—communities have thrived by integrating craftmaking into daily life. By the mid-nineteenth century in Europe, many traditional domestic crafts such as weaving and basketmaking had been taken over by male "professionals" who formed guilds to protect their livelihoods. These guilds were no match for the mighty industrialists, however, and factory-run power looms soon put the cottage industries out of business, essentially eradicating a way of life.

By the early nineteenth century, industrialized labor was the norm, and with the publication of Frederick Winslow Taylor's *Principles of Scientific Management* in 1911, assembly line efficiency was codified. Around the same time the domestic economy (home economics) movement, spearheaded by Christine Frederick, a *Ladies' Home Journal* editor, brought this scientific management into the American home. Advocating the mechanization of kitchens and the streamlining of domestic tasks, Frederick wrote: "The ideal home life today is unhampered by traditions of the past."

Not everyone embraced this as progress. This same period saw the rise of the colonial revival movement, in which many women returned to the handicrafts that had been left behind, forming stitching and weaving societies to make everything from baskets to blankets. At this time the arts-and-crafts movement also elevated craft to a higher plane, advocating handmade furnishings and basket making.

Recent history is rife with this push-pull between man and machine; during times of great leaps in industrial "progress," movements calling for a return to traditional craft and appreciation for handmade objects often rise to the surface. During the postwar boom of the 1950s Alexander Girard, Dorothy Liebes, and Jim Thompson led a revival of interest in traditional crafts, and Girard began amassing the incredible collection of anonymous folk crafts that is now housed at Santa Fe's Museum of International Folk Art. In Japan at the same time, art critic and collector Soetsu Yanagi, along with potters Shoji Hamada and Kanjiro Kawai, formed the Japanese Craft Society. Along with their friend British potter Bernard Leach, these men spearheaded an interest in traditional, handmade crafts that mirrored what was happening on the other side of the world. Yanagi founded the Japan Folk Craft Museum (a must-see if you're ever in Tokyo) to house "the arts of the people, returned to the people."

99

Machines have changed our worlds—whether for better or worse could be debated indefinitely, but the fact remains that almost everything in our homes is made by them. Maybe that's why we sigh as we run our fingers along the rumply edges of a hand-thrown pot; we hardly realize how much our souls long to be surrounded by goods that remember the hands and the heart that made them. Human craftsmanship, in all its glorious inefficiency, will cost us more—and for the discerning wabi-sabi homeowner, that's money well spent.

I slept for years under a duvet cover made from two sheets stitched together, until I could afford a handmade quilt. Then last

Machine-made things are children of the brain; they are not very human. The more they spread, the less the human being is needed. What seems to be a great advance is also a great step backward; the desire for the natural as opposed to the artificial surely has some basic, unchanging significance.

—SOETSU YANAGI

year my husband and I ran across a marvelous quilt shop in a funky old cabin on the shores of Lake Superior in Minnesota. We spent an entire afternoon in the back room with the owner, sifting through calicos and flannels, pulling together just the right combination of sage greens, midnight blues, and rusty reds to create a floating star pattern. We waited for three months as a group of women built our quilt during their weekly bee. When I snuggle under it, I recall the lake's gently lapping waves and feel the solid midwestern women behind those stitches. Honestly, I sleep better knowing it wasn't made by prison labor in Mexico—or a nameless, faceless, soulless machine.

Now my sister Stefanie has learned to quilt, and I envy her talent. She delights in the hunt for vintage bits of cloth, and she pulls them together in ways that astound me. She's devoted an entire room to her craft, and she'll happily invite you in to show you her latest project as well as the Depression-era floral prints she's been collecting for the next one. She is in her element here, and anyone lucky enough to receive one of Stef's quilts gets not only a thing of beauty, but a true gift of love.

 Over the years I've discovered the joy in honoring those whose work I will never match—and learning to love that I don't have to. When I find them, I buy mosaics made by artists with a better eye for design and color than I have. I serve potatoes in an exquisite purple bowl thrown by a potter from my hometown in Iowa. I keep flowers on the kitchen table in an indestructible water jug made by a man I met in Asheville, North Carolina, fired in a kiln powered by methane gas from a landfill. I brew tea in a mustard yellow pot that I picked up during one of the best days I spent in Japan. I'm drawn to all of these things for their beauty and utility, of course, but it's also the people who made them—and the stories behind them —that make the difference to me.

Surrounding myself with the work of talented artisans makes for more than just a beautiful home. It subtly changes the energy in my space, bringing a tiny piece of each craftsperson in with it. Shiho Kanzaki, the extraordinarily talented potter whom I met in Japan, says he believes that spirit and thought are the most important elements in his work. "The making of ceramics and our attitude toward

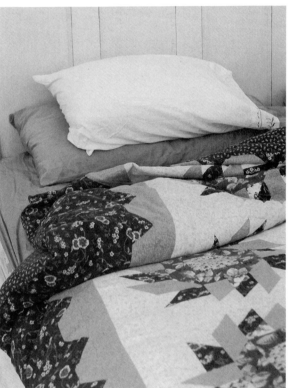

101

living are closely related," he said. "An attitude of disarray toward living can cause us to make works that have a 'wrong spirit' or are without soul." That's one reason I'm always very careful when choosing items for my home, and why I love to meet the artisans who made them, whenever possible. There's never any doubt in my mind when the chemistry is right between me and a piece of pottery—it feels almost carnal. If that involuntary "ooh" doesn't escape from my lips, I probably don't need that certain vase.

If you don't do handcrafts yourself, honor those who do by bringing their wares into your home. This quilt, hand-stitched by a circle of women in northern Minnesota, adds homespun romance to the bedroom.

## THE WABI MASTER

Admiration for rustic, primitive, and handmade wares had been growing in Japan well before tea master Sen no Rikyu brought it to the forefront in the sixteenth century. But no one is more widely credited with bringing the wabi-sabi aesthetic to the masses than he is. His sense of wabi was so highly attuned and so revered, in fact, that his style of tea—wabichado—is still practiced today.

A couple of stories illustrate Rikyu's mastery. Over the years a few different versions with slightly varied details have circulated, but the general thrust remains the same. The first tale goes that when Rikyu was a pupil of Jo-o, his master asked him to tend to his garden. Rikyu cleaned up debris and raked the paths until it was perfect, then scrutinized the immaculate grounds. Before presenting his work, he shook a cherry tree, causing a few blossoms to spill randomly onto the ground.

Later, after he had emerged as Japan's most revered tea master, Rikyu served under Toyotomi Hideyoshi, a warrior known for his ostentatious taste. One day the ruler went to visit Rikyu's famed morning glory garden and was shocked to find it in shambles, all the flowers uprooted. He entered Rikyu's teahouse to find one perfect morning glory in a clay pot. Rikyu could not have proved his point about simple, singular beauty any more elegantly.

When Rikyu acted, the people of Japan listened. One contemporary tea master I spoke with compared him to

Pablo Picasso in the twentieth century; he caused a revolution in thought and perception that made it impossible for the Japanese to return to the old extravagant style of tea. Rikyu downsized the tea hut to one and a half tatami mats and held gatherings by dim sunlight (filtered through bamboo lattice screens) or moonlight. He placed flowers in common fishermen's baskets and commissioned the potter Chojiro to create Raku ceramic tea bowls and replace the fine imported porcelain from China. His overriding goal was to keep everything within the tea hut simple and unembellished, eliminating anything that was unnecessary. For wealthy merchants and samarai, who were used to the more ostentatious style, this created a tense atmosphere that felt like the ultimate luxury—the epitome of high art. For peasants and commoners, it made the art of tea accessible.

One final story proves just how minimalist Rikyu could be. It's said that a poor tea practitioner from the country sent him a large amount of money and asked him to purchase some tea utensils for him because he believed that utensils chosen by Rikyu would greatly elevate his status. He was highly disappointed, however, when Rikyu spent all the money on white cloths and declared, "In the wabi style of tea, even though one owns nothing, if one has only a clean white cloth for wiping the bowl, one is able to drink tea."

## PAINT YOUR OWN

If you're dying to make your creative mark but know you're not likely to be using a pottery wheel or a band saw any time soon, paint-your-own ceramics stores and unfinished furniture shops are a great way to satisfy that muse. Someone else does the hard work of sculpting or building, and you get to have fun with the finishes.

Paint-your-own pottery stores sport shelves of unglazed white ceramic ware, from eggcups to turkey platters. You simply select one, pick out your paint colors, and get to work. You can be as elaborate or as conservative as you want—although I've learned to err on the side of conservatism. (I once made a butter dish with wild squiggly lines and polka dots, and everyone told my five-year-old son what a marvelous job he'd done on it.) The same holds true with unfinished furniture; you can celebrate your artistic flair with bold orange stripes or honor your restrained wabi-sabi taste with a quiet mahogany stain. Whichever way you decide to go, it's infinitely satisfying to spend an afternoon making it work.

Wabi-sabi purists would consider this cheating. The pottery and furniture in these places are mass produced, after all, not *handmade* goods. Those purists probably have the time and energy to hand-plane their wood and dig up their clay, and they should be applauded for that dedication. But if you're an overworked, overscheduled modern American with a yen for a simple creative outlet, you should be applauded for your hand-painted polka-dot egg cups as well.

I honor the craftsmanship of others by bringing their creations into my home—and by using them. "Do people really put flowers in these?" my friend asked Kanzaki-san as we admired the exquisite vases at his studio. "Yes, of course," he answered. "The flowers are what make them beautiful." It would sadden him, he told us, to see his vases displayed like trophies on shelves, never reaching their full glory as a vessel for nature's gifts.

Later, we ate soba noodles with Kanzaki-san and his wife in a weathered Shigaraki teahouse, on pottery made by his apprentices. Before each course, we stopped to admire the shape, the texture, the markings left by ash when the bowl or plate was fired. The rustic acorn-colored bowls embraced the lightly battered shrimp and the hot broth as the noodles swirled in on themselves. Steam rose from thick, dark cups holding strong green tea. There's no doubt in my mind that this pottery enhanced the food's flavor.

For American sculptor Kiki Smith, much of the beauty inherent in pottery is this ability to interact with it. "The owner acts with it in a direct way: own it, use it," she says. "In that way it is like jewelry. One doesn't simply stand back and observe and admire as one is likely to do with a painting or sculpture. Ceramic objects must be used."

I believe this is the case with all handmade household wares; they inspire our own creativity as we consider how best to honor them with our use. Keeping the North Carolina water jug on my kitchen table forces me to plant myself in the season by filling it with a few fresh flowers or branches. I'm more likely to spend some time arranging and garnishing side dishes before I serve them in my

Handcraftsmanship, if it be alive, justifies itself at any time as an intimate expression of the spirit of man. Such work is an end in itself and not a means to an end. If, however, it ceases to serve a functional need, it runs the risk of becoming art for art's sake and untrue to its nature.

—BERNARD LEACH

105

✳ purple bowl from Iowa. I love to fluff my hand-stitched Minnesota quilt and pull it up taut over the bed; I get to admire it all day, and it's that much more inviting to crawl under at night.

How much more pleasant would drying dishes be if you could use a thick, densely stitched hand-knit dishcloth? Might you be less likely to let a wastebasket woven of willow branches overflow with trash? Have you ever swept the floor with a handcrafted broom made from real broomcorn? It has tiny spurs that trap and hold dust, whereas plastic bristles rely on static electricity. These are the tools of our everyday lives. If we choose them wisely, our everyday lives will be that much more beautiful and meaningful.

106

Preparing food—with or without handcrafted pottery to serve it on —is an ideal way to hone your creative flair and bring a sense of beauty into your home. You have to do it every day, anyway—and if you stop to recognize the simple majesty of the objects you bring home in grocery bags, making dinner will be a lot more fun.

Next time you unload the groceries, particularly the produce, do so mindfully. Notice the fine white hairs protecting the carrot's flesh, the squeaky wax binding the cheese wedge, the chunky shapes or fine straight bands of different pastas. How can you make the most of crisp spring greens, plump August tomatoes, golden fall pumpkins? You can toss them, mash them, and spice them up for consumption, of course, and you can also use them to add seasonal grace to the dining table. Pile lettuce leaves in a rustic wooden trough, accentuate the tomatoes' deep red by placing them in a bright yellow bowl, line up the pumpkins so they march down

Cooking is just as creative and imaginative an activity as drawing, or wood carving, or music.

—JULIA CHILD

the middle of a long trestle table. I have a friend who calls this "food art."

I learned in Japan that the deliciousness of food lies as much in presentation as in preparation. Japanese food itself is simple— generally fish, rice, vegetables, maybe some seaweed or vinegar—but it is spectacular when the golden brown edges of the pan-seared hake pick up the rusty flecks of the platter it's on, or when just the right amount of inky black seaweed strings have been tucked on top as garnish. Five thin slices of raw tuna and a dab of bright green wasabi become a masterpiece when fanned on an opalescent shell-shaped plate. In the heat of summer, a smooth, thin square of chilled tofu, floating on chunks of half-melted ice in a shallow bamboo bowl, is appetizing and refreshing. Every time I was presented with one of these dishes, I felt like I was being handed a great gift— something well beyond mere sustenance.

Okita Matsuura, a well-known Japanese chef from Akaina City, explains it this way: "Japan has four seasons, and each season has its own flavors, with an abundance of all sorts of delicacies from the land and sea on the market. Making Japanese food involves expressing those flavors in the food and, at the same time, satisfying the taste buds. There is probably no more delicate cuisine in the world than Japanese cuisine. The unique flavors, serving

107

Old-fashioned utensils are often just as efficient—and provide more opportunity for contemplation—than electric appliances.

methods, and ways in which dishes are used are completely different from those found in any other cuisine. The ingredients must be very carefully selected, and then prepared so as to bring to life their natural flavors. The tradition of Japanese cuisine is, 'value the presentation as well as the flavor.'"

I believe the cook benefits from thoughtful, artful food preparation as well. When I'm making dinner, I often experience the same meditative mindset that my boss, Linda, talks about finding when she weaves. At the end of a crazy day full of too much to do, I love the rich smell of wine-laced beef stew simmering slowly over a low flame, the squish of hamburger between my fingers as I mold together a meatloaf, the snapping and popping of battered chicken crackling in hot oil. As the late afternoon sun bathes my kitchen, my knife scrapes the cutting board and I lift the heavy cast-iron lid to check the sauce just one more time. Rushing is not an option here; this is a place to practice patience, to savor anticipation.

Christy Bartlett, a wabi aesthete who teaches tea in San Francisco, shares my predilection for these culinary gifts. She says she loves thinking about the different shapes she's making as she cuts vegetables, considering whether to make them long and narrow or short and chunky. "It's simple and perhaps simpleminded," she admits, "but sometimes we need to be that way. And the kitchen is a place where we can develop a sense of the combination of aesthetics and function, pay attention to the small moments of life. If you can find great beauty in the small moments, there's no greater gift you can find."

108

A couple of years ago, I heard Diane Ackerman, who writes beautifully about gardens and gardening, discussing her passion on National Public Radio. She and the host agreed that our gardens reflect our selves, our way of looking at life. I thought about my own garden, and I liked the idea. My lavender was just plumping with sweet-smelling buds, the vinca was fresh and green with perky purple flowers, and the peonies held promise in their tight little fists.

That was in June. By August, the thought of my wild, out-of-control garden reflecting anything about me was slightly horrifying. The lemon balm had run amok; the peony bush—never caged —was limp and trampled. In my backyard, a virulent type of Japanese knotweed had grown into a jungle. As it does every year, nature had taken its course in my yard, and I hadn't managed to keep it in check. Oh, the temptation to just call it wabi-sabi and leave it at that. It was, after all, very *natural* in its untidy way.

But I know better. Wabi-sabi is tamed, subdued, and serene. I know that the natural gardens I inevitably fall for—which feel almost untouched by human hands—actually owe their serenity and peace to hours of hard labor. There's a fine art to creating a garden that feels close to nature but also offers carefully thought-out spots for meditation and reflection, just the right combination of color and blooms throughout the season, and enough structure and muscle to provide interest even in December. A truly wabi-sabi garden is a creative endeavor of the highest sort. And some day— when my kids are older and my work life slows down—I vow I'll accomplish that.

Just cultivate delight. Enjoy the sensory pleasures of the garden. That's number one.

—DIANE ACKERMAN

109

# chabana

I can hear tea master Gary Cadwallader's voice in my head every time I think about writing the word *arrangement* in conjunction with the flowers used in the tearoom. "We do not *arrange* flowers," he reminds me again and again. To be truly wabi, flowers are simply placed, in their most natural form, into vessels that enhance their beauty.

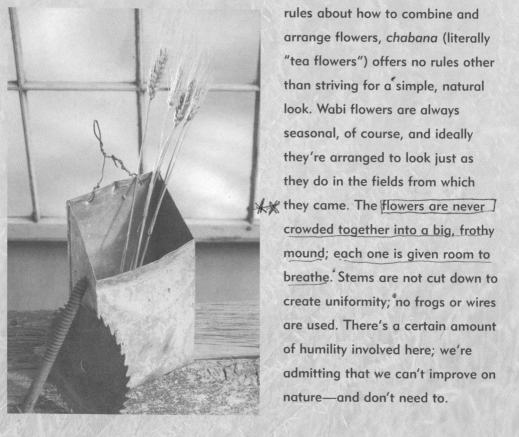

Unlike *ikebana*, which sets forth pretty stringent, stylized rules about how to combine and arrange flowers, *chabana* (literally "tea flowers") offers no rules other than striving for a simple, natural look. Wabi flowers are always seasonal, of course, and ideally they're arranged to look just as they do in the fields from which they came. The flowers are never crowded together into a big, frothy mound; each one is given room to breathe. Stems are not cut down to create uniformity; no frogs or wires are used. There's a certain amount of humility involved here; we're admitting that we can't improve on nature—and don't need to.

If you fiddle this
way and that with
the flowers and
consequently they
wither, that will be no
benefit. It is the same
with a person's life.

—SEN SOSHITSU XV

Minimalism is key. Instead of the typically blowsy display of a dozen English roses, try one wild rose in a bud vase. Pick a few stems of the chicory growing between the cracks in the sidewalk and let them settle into an old bottle. Work with single flowers or small, odd numbers. Forget about flowers altogether and use a solitary branch (bare in midwinter, budding in springtime) or a few tall grasses. Eschew elaborate cut-crystal vases for humble containers: baskets, bamboo slices, hollowed gourds.

Those who've been intimidated by the art of flower *arranging* can breathe a sigh of relief; wabi flowers require no special training or talent. They simply ask for an honest eye, a willingness to observe what's growing right outside your door and not mess with it as you bring it in (leaving things alone tends to be the hardest part for most people). The art of wabi flowers lies in letting go of our preconceived notions of what flower *arrangements* must be. Who says peonies are only beautiful when they're in bloom? Who says tulips in their final yawning moments are no longer fit for display? Who says dandelions are weeds? (Think about your childhood instincts; how many times did you pick a bouquet of these sunny blossoms and bring it home to your mother?)

You can hone your wabi flower "skills" by designating a space in your home that you vow to keep filled with flora that you've gathered from within a one-mile radius of where you live. In spring, when the world is crawling with fresh blooms, and in fall, when colors are crisp and crackling, this will be a cakewalk. It's harder in summer, believe it or not; the obvious choices such as daylilies and daisies are everywhere, but most of the trees and bushes sport somewhat monotonous green foliage. Winter offers the best wabi possibilities: dried grasses and seedpods and naked, sculptural twigs and branches. Just remember: You are not arranging these finds. You're simply transferring them to a new home.

For an easy way to bring wabi-sabi into your décor, display seasonally appropriate wildflowers in found objects such as baskets, gourds, or old bottles. Instead of cutting them to make the display perfectly symmetrical, arrange them to reflect their relative heights and natural disposition. To be truly wabi-sabi, the *chabana* should include an odd number of flowers, and the stems should not be crowded.

I'm slowly working toward my wabi-sabi paradise by putting in
plants that are <u>native</u> to my place: slightly weedy black-eyed Susans
and columbine, wild rosebushes dug up from my neighbor's yard,
heat-loving yarrow. I've welcomed intruders, if they have something
to offer and don't get too pushy. The chokecherry that made its way
down from the foothills near my house—home to its many cousins
and uncles—provides long, delicate white blossoms in springtime
and brilliant red-orange leaves in the fall (great branches to bring
inside). The mullein that planted itself in my flower garden is tough
and phallic, but the bloom of tiny yellow flowers around its stalk in
late summer belies its feminine side.

113

These indigenous species, adapted to my brutal high-desert climate, can take care of themselves and manage to look good—even
in August—without a lot of care and attention. The creative part,
for me, is mapping out where they'll thrive and how they'll interact
with each other and with the humans who visit. And this is where
the wabi-sabi spirit really comes in. The wabi-sabi garden embraces
and enhances the delicate balance between nature and nurture. It's
not formal and fussy like an English garden—but it's also not over-
run with lemon balm and knotweed. Plants are chosen because they
belong in that garden, in that climate. They're allowed to strut their
stuff, but they're expected to be considerate of the plants around
them—or be tamed. Brash, blowsy blooms, which generally require
a high degree of maintenance, are used sparingly, if at all.

Just as important as what plants are chosen and where they're
placed are the garden's bones: the stones and <u>pebbles</u> used to create
winding paths and delineations, the <u>rusty iron gate</u> beckoning

entrance, the trellis teasing vines up its length. In this aspect, gardens offer all sorts of wabi-sabi opportunity. Place an old, broken-down chair in the flowerbeds; let the weather work its magic and the plants grow up around it until it seems rooted and organic to that place. Plant gourds in an old wheelbarrow and let them spill languidly over the sides. Build a stone wall; the very act of placing stone upon stone is a satisfying meditation. Create paths that encourage guests to meander, with stopping points where the vista is ideal.

114

With the right structure in place, the wabi-sabi garden is as beautiful—if not more so—in December as it is in June. The sculptural bare branches, brittle seedpods, and somber palette of the winter garden are as wabi-sabi as it gets. Stark and naked, the plants stand as vivid symbols of nature's way: birth, death, rebirth. The blossoms of life are easy to admire; the quiet integrity of plants gathering energy for rebirth takes a deeper appreciation. A stroll through the garden in the dead of winter is a fine place to cultivate that depth.

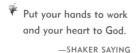
Put your hands to work and your heart to God.
—SHAKER SAYING

Could be that I'm about to go too far here. A section about *housekeeping* under the heading "Create"? Come on . . . what could possibly be creative about housekeeping?

Lots, really. Every time you sweep, dust, or clear away clutter, you're creating clean, sacred—wabi—space. One of the ancient tea masters, in fact, described *wabisuki* (a taste for all things wabi) as "putting one's whole heart to cleaning and repeating it several times." Wabi housekeeping is about so much more than just sponging and mopping; it's about creating rituals that facilitate caring for your home and nurturing those who live within. And, as the Dalai Lama has pointed out, cleansing your environment is a ritual means of also cleansing your mind.

## THE WABI-SABI CLEANING CUPBOARD

You can invoke the wab-sabi spirit of simplicity and old-fashioned wisdom every time you clean your home by using basic ingredients you may already have in your kitchen or medicine cabinet.

**HYDROGEN PEROXIDE** to remove mold and disinfect

**CLUB SODA** to clean and shine fixtures and windows

**VINEGAR** to cut grease, lime deposits, soap buildup; deodorize toilet; remove film on floors

**BAKING SODA** to scour and remove smudges or scuffs

**CLUB SODA** to clean windows

**BORAX** to deodorize, disinfect, and inhibit mold growth

**LEMON JUICE** to remove grease and tarnish

**SALT** mixed with water to destroy bacteria

**BAKING SODA** with vinegar rinse for stainless steel

**OLIVE OIL** to polish furniture (mix 3 parts oil to 1 part vinegar for a cleaner shine)

More practically, you can add creativity and care to your cleaning rituals by taking a good look at the cleaning products you're using. You could go buy them off the shelves at the grocery store, as long as you're not all that concerned about bringing caustic, toxic chemicals into your home. Or you could make creative use of simple, everyday ingredients such as baking soda, vinegar, and lemon to clean and shine without risking your own or your family's health. Vinegar cuts grease and deodorizes, baking soda scours and removes smudges, and club soda shines up windows. Adding a little lemon or essential oil to any of these makes your cleaning all the more pleasant.

Like cooking, housekeeping is one of those tasks that there's no getting out of—so you might as well make it as pleasant as possible. Again, you can turn it into a meditation, and you can take pride in what you're doing. Don't just clean up, but add your own thoughtful touches. Soak a cotton ball in vanilla and place it in your closet to freshen up your clothes. Pour some vinegar into a small bowl and place it on a high shelf to absorb kitchen odors. Add some lavender essential oil when you throw clothes into the washing machine. Iron the sheets with a little starch.

Try to change your attitude toward cleaning your home from one of drudgery to one of creative challenge. Focus on the tasks at hand with the kind of concentration you would bring any creative endeavor. And when you're finished, always allow yourself a moment to sit and bask in the fruits of this wabisuki: the crisp smell of freshly laundered sheets, the sun beaming through streak-less windows, the amber glow of polished wood.

There, now . . . how can you not feel creative?

**COLLAGES.** Start out by just collecting bits and pieces that appeal to you: magazine and newspaper clippings, dried flowers, pressed leaves, bits of wrapping paper. Keep it all in a box and when you're feeling creative, sort through it and begin combining it on paper. You might just be amazed at what results. Recently I met a woman in Austin, Texas, who created a monumental variation on this theme. Her stone garden wall is encrusted with shells, religious metals, bits of old jewelry, and other odds and ends that she'd collected for years. This spectacular enclosure stops passersby in their tracks; it's great fun to watch people slow down and discover the quirky odds and ends as they walk by.

**DRIED FLOWERS.** Nothing could be simpler than this one. Stop throwing out your flowers once they've passed their prime. Hang them upside down in a closet for a week or two (depending on what kind of climate you live in) and let them dry. Then let your imagination run wild. Fill a tarnished silver bowl with tiny dried rosebuds and place it in the bathroom; use the flowers instead of bows when you wrap packages; include a few petals when you send cards or letters.

**AN INDOOR ROCK GARDEN.** Whenever a pebble or small stone catches your fancy, pick it up and put it in your pocket. Place these in a small frame on your desk, and arrange, then rearrange to suit your whims. It's a great thing to do when you need a moment to relax.

Chapter 5

# the sound of silence

# listen

In describing his idyllic days at Walden Pond, Henry David Thoreau tells of summer mornings spent sitting in his sunny doorway until noon, "in undisturbed solitude and stillness, while the birds sang amid or flittered noiseless through the house, until by the sun falling in at my west window, or the noise of some traveler's wagon on the distant highway, I was reminded of the lapse of time."

Wouldn't it be lovely? For most of us the thought of frittering away half a day sitting in a doorway is laughable at best. But let's say the miraculous occurs, and we find ourselves with an unscheduled morning and a doorway bathed in sunlight. Would we actually

O Great Spirit, help me always . . . to remember the peace that may be found in silence.

—CHEROKEE PRAYER

119

find the kind of Thoreauvian quiet that could be broken by the squeak of wagon wheels making their slow, low-tech journey across a distant road? How distant would the road even be? Would we be serenaded by birdsong or by the roar of jet planes overhead? Might the reminder of lapsed time be the beeping of our own PalmPilot?

We live noisy lives. We drive machines that choke and zoom and pierce the air with their car alarms. The inescapable ring of telephones is a constant in our homes, in our offices, even while we watch our kids play soccer. Music accompanies us as we drive, shop, and eat. The roar of planes overhead is incessant. Highways have become high-speed expressways. Smaller lots with bigger houses mean we get an earful of Emeril whenever the neighbors kick up the volume on their stereo television. Lawn mowers, chain saws, and barking dogs add to the hubbub.

Thunder was the loudest noise that rocked the world of pre-industrial humans. Back before internal combustion, roars and booms signaled danger, and our bodies still react to loud noises with a prehistoric adrenaline surge: our hearts pump harder, our blood pressure rises, our blood vessels constrict. Living in a din of electronic toots and beeps, mechanical grinding and grumbling, unrelenting amplified music, and blaring loudspeakers, it's no wonder we're stressed.

Former U.S. Surgeon General William H. Stewart recognized this back in 1968, when he declared, "Calling noise a nuisance is like calling smog an inconvenience. Noise must be considered a hazard to the health of people everywhere." Endocrine, cardiovascular, and immune systems can all suffer from chronic noise, and children from highly noisy households have been found to experience delayed language skills and increased anxiety. Noise disturbs sleep, affects emotional well-being, and may contribute to heart disease and mental illness.

Noise has been an issue for as long as humans have lived in civilizations. In 6000 BC the Sybarites banned blacksmiths and cabinetmakers, with their bang-bang-banging, from working in residential areas. Julius Caesar tried to put an end to the clamor of speeding chariots over cobblestones. And in some cities in medieval Europe, horse carriages and horseback riding were not allowed at night; straw was strewn on the streets to muffle the sound of hooves and wheels by day. Inside the homes of the upper classes, thick tapestries and straw on the floors protected aristocratic ears from the eternal noise of hawkers and street musicians.

Modern living has made urban noise a much bigger problem than our ancestors ever could have imagined. Who could have predicted that in a modern version of straw and tapestries, Queen Elizabeth would ban cell phone use in Buckingham Palace? Over the past fifteen years the noise level in major metropolitan areas has increased sixfold; urban noise doubles every eight to ten years. The New York City Police Department's Quality of Life hotline logs more noise complaints by far than any other. And across the nation, noise is Americans' number one complaint about their neighborhoods, the most cited reason for moving, according to the 2000 census.

Yet even in the unpopulated wilderness, where cell phones don't work and no one's found a way to pipe in Muzak, noise is unavoidable. In 1998 Gordon Hempton, a sound recordist attempting to build a library of natural sounds, toured fifteen states west of the Mississippi and found only two areas—in the mountains of Colorado and the Boundary Waters of Minnesota—that were free of motors, aircraft, industrial clamor, or gunfire for more than fifteen minutes during daylight. I discovered this myself last year, during a women's retreat in the Rocky Mountains. One afternoon our leaders sent us all off in different directions with pencil and paper, to find a tranquil spot and record what we heard. Apparently I was pretty far from the quiet piece of Colorado that Gordon Hempton had managed to find. "Airplane," I wrote. "Airplane. Airplane. Airplane. Helicopter." Then finally, blessedly, "Mosquito."

The wabi-sabi home should be a quiet refuge, perhaps the only place where we can escape to nurture what Quakers call "the still, small voice within." Yet most of us have probably quit noticing the constant bumps and grinds inside our homes: the humming of the refrigerator and the air conditioner, the low roar of the heater gearing up, the startling thunk of the washing machine's automatic water shutoff, the high-pitched whirr of the electric coffee grinder, the beeps and bloops of the computer. With the advent of sonic technology, even our toothbrushes are loud.

I try to listen to the still, small voice within but I can't hear it above the din

—ELIZA WARD, FROM *LITTLE AUDREY'S STORY*

Our preferences for open floor plans, with rooms merging into one another through wide doorless passageways or waist-high walls, allow sound to bounce freely around our houses. The popular great room connects everything to the kitchen—the loudest room in the house.

Our eardrums suffer because modern construction does much less to block sound than buildings of old. Gypsum board, the wallboard of choice since World War II, absorbs much less sound than the inch-thick plaster walls used in prewar buildings. Most interior walls today have sound transmission class ratings of about 30, a level at which loud speech can be heard through the wall. Old-fashioned cast-iron pipes were denser, and thus quieter, than the plastic pipes used today.

In addition, outside noise seeps into the home through windows, holes in walls, and wooden framework. Alone, "background noise" from planes, car horns, voices, and music averages fifty to sixty decibels—about equal to the decibel level of an air conditioner in use—in the typical urban home. Can our homes really be a wabi-sabi refuge amid the clamor of the modern world? The answer is decidedly yes.

123

Not all sound is annoying or unwelcome. Our homes also ring with laughter, children at play, celebration, and music (without which, Plato said, "the soul becomes feeble, deaf, and blind"). We're soothed by the gentle patter of rain on the windows, and we want to be able to throw those windows open to hear the sparrows come spring. Even Thoreau welcomed the sound of church bells on Sunday, "a faint, sweet, and, as it were, natural melody worth importing into the wilderness."

The sound quality in our homes is just as important as the visual landscape we create. Yet R. Murray Schafer, a Canadian musician who developed the concept of "acoustic ecology," believes

The ears are the most intimate organs of the soul.

—THOMAS MOORE

that in our "eye culture," we've forgotten how to listen. He suggests fine-tuning your ears through "soundwalks," in which you simply walk and listen for about an hour. Repeat the walk at different times of the year and listen to the change of seasons: the return of the robins, the whistle of autumn wind, the silence of a blanket of snow. When you return home, write down your experiences. Or keep a sound journal, a daily record of what you hear. Through this, the voice of your home will emerge. Had you noticed how loudly that grandfather clock ticks? Or how loudly the dog snores?

The goal, of course, is to bring more of the good noise into your home and find ways to eliminate the bad. The first part's pretty easy: tickle your kids, tell more jokes, buy a few good CDs, play your piano, hang wind chimes. Be careful with the "acoustical perfume," however. Too many wind chimes, or chimes that are too large for your space, will simply add to the din. Also consider placement. I gave my mom a fountain when she moved from the country into the city a few years ago. She set it up near her bed . . . for one sleepless night.

If your home is particularly loud—especially in rooms such as the bedroom, home office, or meditation space, where quiet is not just a luxury but a priority—you could bring in a white noise generator. Small enough to fit into the palm of your hand, these devices produce gentle rushing sounds that help mask traffic noise and voices. Pink noise generators are a bit more intrusive, with ocean, rain, and waterfall sounds. These devices aren't traditionally wabi-sabi, but sometimes modern ingenuity is the only answer in an industrial world.

Bookshelves not only control clutter but they also help soundproof a room. The walnut wood in these shelves, ingeniously designed to include drawer space, is from a farm owned by the homeowner's uncle in southeast Oklahoma.

125

Noise abatement ranks right up there with improving energy efficiency and designing products for reliability.

—NORMAN REMICH, EDITOR, *APPLIANCE MANUFACTURER*

126

A couple of years ago we ripped out the grimy carpet on our stairs and in our hallway and replaced it with hardwood floors. Aesthetically and sanitarily, it's a huge improvement; the wood is smooth and golden, and the floor is no longer a trap for dog hair and dust. What we hadn't counted on was the difference in noise level. Footsteps and voices clatter and bang, with nothing to absorb their impact. Conversations echo through the hallway in a way they didn't before.

That carpet, for its many flaws, had done a lot to mitigate the noise in our house. The new hardwood floors, for their many virtues, now act as big drumheads. Sound bounces off of them and reverberates throughout the house. The same is true of bare walls (especially if they're plaster) and plain wood furniture. Experts say the only way to minimize this effect is to make sure that at least 25 percent of a room contains some absorbent material such as drapes, venetian blinds, fabric wall hangings, large canvas paintings, or carpet. Book-filled bookcases and deep, soft upholstered furniture—the softer and larger, the better—will also help stop sound from bouncing around the room.

But wait a minute now. Are thick pile carpets and plush, overstuffed armchairs wabi-sabi? Maybe we've hit a wall with this wabi-sabi thing. Can we really have it all—the stark, rustic wabi-sabi aesthetic as well as peace and quiet? Sure, we can. If we're careful about the sound-absorbing materials we choose.

Back in 1918, beleaguered by the sound of revelers below his Paris apartment, Marcel Proust lined his entire bedroom with cork so he could complete *Remembrance of Things Past* (a technique

now referred to as "Prousting"). Cork, made from the bark of cork oak trees, is a great sound-absorbing material because 50 percent of its molecular structure is air; it's also dark and earthy-looking and has an appealing, albeit funky, smell. Use it for floors and also to line the inside of cupboards and drawers, which will prevent clanging as you put away dishes and silverware.

The trick to giving your home the wabi-sabi quiet treatment is to find sound-absorbing materials that remain primitive in nature. It's not all that difficult. When considering drapes, look for nubby hemp, rustic burlap, or mohair instead of velvet or damask. Avoid synthetic carpet in never-from-nature colors and, instead, look for carpet made from natural materials such as sisal, jute, seagrass, or unbleached wool. For added sound protection on walls, consider panels of burlap-covered Homasote, a sound-deadening fiberboard made from recycled newspapers.

Also take a close look at your appliances—it's easier than ever to find quiet ones. GE, KitchenAid, Modern Maid, Sears, Thermador, and Whirlpool all make dishwashers that include "quiet" features, and KitchenAid and Sears offer insulation material for retrofitting existing machines. Miele claims its vacuum cleaner is so quiet that you can talk on the phone while using it.

127

These antique mohair curtains, rescued from a Victorian home in Wyoming, not only add wabi-sabi charm, but they also provide valuable soundproofing against noises outside.

## SOUNDPROOFING: THE ADVANCED COURSE

The following noise control techniques rank from small, quick fixes to major projects. If you don't mind a little noise, you'll find more than enough satisfaction with the quick fixes. If you're highly sensitive to noise or live near an airport or a highway, across the street from a fire station, or anywhere in New York City, you might want to take a closer look at the bigger projects. Taking a look doesn't mean you actually have to get out a hammer and caulk gun, however. It simply means you have options if the noise level starts to get to you.

### QUICK FIXES

- Place half-inch-thick pads of rubber or cork under the legs or corners of large heavy appliances such as washing machines, dryers, and refrigerators to stop vibrations from transferring to the floor.
- Move appliances at least two inches away from the wall.
- Place rubber pads under small appliances, dish racks, on countertops near the stove, and in sink basins.
- Put stereo speakers on stands to prevent turning floors or walls into whole-house speakers. Alternatively, place rubber vibration isolator mats, available from office supply, computer or audio equipment stores, beneath speakers and computer printers.
- Install rubber or cork tile on cabinet walls and shelves.

## CRACKS AND CREVICES

Sealing any small opening through which air and noise can enter a room is the cheapest, fastest, and most efficient way to block noise. You can test for sound leaks by darkening a room to see where light—and therefore sound—is seeping in.

- Caulk or seal all cracks or openings in walls and doors.
- Seal holes around electrical service entrances, vents, steam or water pipes, and air conditioners—any gap where sound can sneak in.
- Remove the faceplates from electrical outlets and switches and caulk the spaces between the box and the wall.
- Remove baseboards and seal the space between the walls and the floors with caulking compound.
- Remove recessed light fixtures from the ceiling, seal the holes with wallboard and spackling compound, and replace with track or soffit lighting.

## INSULATION

- Line the cavities that hold the dishwasher, refrigerator, and trash compactor with sound-absorbing materials.
- Insulate attic and walls.
- Add mass to walls with a second layer of drywall. Place the second layer as a "floating wall," apart from the first, to create an air space baffle. The thicker the space, the more effective the barrier.

## WINDOWS

- Invest in double-glazed windows. They provide noticeably improved soundproofing because of the air cavity between the two panes.
- In really loud areas, consider double windows with a large air gap. Place acoustic absorbent material on the perimeter reveal around the gap.
- Caulk existing windows and equip them with gaskets to provide an airtight seal.
- Install storm windows with heavy glass and high-quality weather stripping.
- Place shutters inside the window so that you can close out noise from indoors.

## DOORS

- Install a storm door.
- Replace hollow-core doors with solid doors. If that's not possible, add an extra surface of plywood to both sides of the door to help absorb more sound.
- Place weather stripping around all doors, even interior ones. Replace any weather stripping that's loose or admits light or air.
- Use flexible rubber threshold seals to close off the space below doors.
- Cover up the mail slot if it's practical to do so.

## PLUMBING AND MECHANICAL SYSTEMS

- Insulate plastic pipes to minimize gurgling and sloshing.
- Install water hammer arresters, available at hardware stores, to absorb the shock of copper pipes clunking when the washing machine or dishwasher valves quickly shut off the water supply. Whole-system hammer arresters can be soldered into the water line; individual appliance arresters simply screw on.
- Tune up the furnace: lubricate the blower, replace filters, check belts and pulleys for wear.

## LANDSCAPING

- Plant trees and hedges. At the very least, they provide psychological relief by blocking noise sources from view.
- Conifers and broad-leaved evergreens are the most effective year-round noise blockers.
- Install a barrier wall or fence with a solid, continuous surface. It should be tall enough to hide the entire roadway from the house.
- Mask noise with fountains, waterfalls, or tall ornamental grasses that make a soothing sound when the wind blows.
- Replace electric or motorized leaf blowers, lawn mowers, and hedge trimmers with old-fashioned rakes, push mowers, and clippers.

To my mind, the idea that doing dishes is unpleasant can occur only when you are not doing them. . . . I enjoy taking my time with each dish, being fully aware of the dish, the water, and each movement of my hands.

—THICH NHAT HANH

132

In our rush for convenience—it's fair to say "need," in today's busy world—we've motorized nearly every household task. Before I'm even out of bed, I hear my husband pulverizing coffee beans in the electric grinder. After showering, I blow-dry my hair, brush my teeth with my sonic toothbrush, then make myself a breakfast smoothie in the blender. Over the course of the day, I whisk the dog hair off my floors with a Dirt Devil and pile loads of clothes into the washing machine and dryer. I make dinner using a little electric chopper for onions and a food processor for the big stuff, then stack my dirty dishes in the dishwasher. The stereo plays Billie Holiday, while my son's computer games make digital dialogue. And I consider my house relatively low-tech: we don't even have an electric can opener or a trash compactor.

All of this noise robs us of opportunities to bring contemplation into our daily lives. In Zen Buddhism *samu,* or manual labor, is viewed as an opportunity to quiet, deepen, and energize our minds. In most Zen monasteries, mornings are spent sweeping, dusting, scrubbing, and gardening. For thousands of years, writes Roshi Philip Kapleau in *The Three Pillars of Zen,* "manual labor has been an essential ingredient of Zen discipline."

"To work is to pray," said the Benedictine monks. The Amish understand this as well. Contrary to what many believe, Amish culture doesn't reject "progress" out of hand, but it carefully weighs whether each new technology will truly enhance and improve all aspects of their lives. In most cases, they've found that the trade-off of expense, noise, and planned obsolescence isn't worth the value of being present with a task.

Think about the difference between filling your space with the roar of the vacuum cleaner's engine and the whisper of straw against the floor as you make strokes with a broom. The satisfaction of a knife slicing through the crisp flesh of an onion, its strong smell permeating your senses, versus the sterile whirr of a machine shredding it to bits. Fifteen minutes spent outside, under the influence of fresh air and sunlight, pinning clothes to a line.

When I was growing up, my family had a KitchenAid, and it was most efficient for my sisters and I to simply divide up the nights and take on the kitchen cleanup duty alone. But I remember Thanksgivings at my grandmother's, a place without a dishwasher, where the women would gather in the kitchen and divide into sudsers, rinsers, and dryers. As the china passed from one hand to another, conversations—the ones that didn't take place at the mixed-gender dinner table—flowed. For me, this female bonding was as much a part of the Thanksgiving ritual as my grandma's mincemeat pie.

Perhaps this seemed so magical to me because it was a novelty; had my sisters and I been forced to wash all the dinner dishes by hand every night we'd certainly have resented missing the latest

133

Every once in a while, forego the mechanical and accomplish household tasks by hand. Washing the dishes provides an opportunity for meditation and relieves your kitchen of the dishwasher's noisy cycles.

episode of *Charlie's Angels*. These modern conveniences were invented for a reason, and they've been invaluable in freeing women from housework so they could spread their wings in the wider world. To be honest, I'd be far less likely to make my son's favorite eggplant pasta dish as often if I had to chop the onions by hand every single time.

I know we'd be nuts to patently give up the machines that permeate our homes and make our lives so much easier. But what if, every once in a while—especially when the world around us seems crazy and uncontrollable—we submerge our hands into warm, soapy water and hand a towel to our significant other (that person we've resorted to e-mailing and leaving cell phone messages about who's picking up the kids and who's dropping off the drycleaning). Or we take ten minutes to sweep the floor, focusing all our attention on that simple task with its ancient symbolic reference to sweeping away the bad spirits and the stale energy that may be lurking in the corners. What if?

In the end, the most important piece of quieting our homes is not soundproofing materials or quieter kitchen appliances but rather how we live our lives within them. This really came home to me during a conversation with Arline Bronzaft, who has conducted several studies on how noise affects children. "I live on the Upper East Side," Arline said to me. "Do I have doubled-glazed windows? Yes. I'm not a fool. But what makes a home quiet is the people who live there."

134

In the attitude of silence the soul finds the path in a clearer light, and what is elusive and deceptive resolves itself into crystal clearness.

—MAHATMA GANDHI

In her research, Arline has found that high academic achievers grow up in homes where TVs, stereo systems, and computers are not often blaring and where quiet dinnertime gatherings offer ample opportunity for conversation. "A noisy, cluttered home doesn't foster parent-child interaction," Arline said. "Yet we've created households that don't value and esteem quiet and serenity. This is important not just for mental health and learning, but for spirit and soul."

Many of us find silence intimidating. We equate it with boredom or fear that tuning out would mean losing touch with the outside world. In a loud culture, our own ability to fill the space with more noise and louder music makes us feel strong and powerful. Those of us who grew up in a world of pervasive FM are soothed by the familiar lull of background music; losing that can be frightening. In fact, a Yahoo! News survey conducted in 2000 found that almost half of all respondents aged eighteen to twenty-four said they would not go without music for one week, even for $1,000.

Emotions and feelings tend to rise to the surface in a silent pool; many of us aren't quite sure we want to face that. I know that when I'm bothered about something, I'm much more likely to crank up my favorite Gourds CD while I'm in the car—loud enough for people in the car behind me to sing along. Arline Bronzaft believes many people turn on the television the minute they walk through the door and leave it on until they go to bed because "they're afraid to be in touch with themselves."

## JUST SIT

Lots of people had suggested meditation to me; my mind is loud and cluttered, and it shows. But I'm so busy, I always muttered. Much too busy to just *sit there doing nothing* for twenty minutes each day. And then one winter, my thoughts became so crowded that I had to give this meditation thing a try.

I read books about Zen Buddhism. These all described *zazen*, or sitting Zen, as the practice of sitting in lotus position (legs crisscrossed), with a straight spine and upright head, eyes slightly open, lowered, and unfocused, emptying the mind of all thoughts and focusing all attention on the breath as it enters and leaves the body.

Seemed simple enough. I vowed to sit, for five minutes a day. I mean, really, who couldn't make their mind shut up for five short minutes?

Well, I couldn't. No matter how hard I tried to stop my thoughts, there they were. And when I tried to label those thoughts "thinking" and let them go—as the books told me to do—there were plenty more right on their heels. I thought I might be incapable of quieting my mind—ever. But I read in Shunryu Suzuki's book, *Zen Mind, Beginners' Mind*, that "the result is not the point; it is the effort

Creating a private meditation space is a means of honoring yourself that you won't regret. You don't have to follow any prescribed rules; simply fill the space with items that hold meaning for you.

to improve ourselves that is valuable." And so each day I sat on my cushion and became very aware of how much I think.

"There is no particular way in true practice," Suzuki assures readers, so I took his advice and moved on to other guidebooks. And I found so many ways to meditate. You can focus your attention on a specific object (a candle flame works for me) or chant (*om* became popular because many meditation teachers believe a word ending in *m* or *n* is most helpful). You can count, and when daydreaming interrupts, simply start again. In the practice of *japa*, Hindus use counting beads, similar to Catholic rosaries, as they repeat their divine word or mantra. In discourse meditation, the mind follows passing emotions and thoughts without guiding them or labeling them "good" and "bad."

For those who just can't sit still, there's walking meditation or yoga, which quiets and connects us through postures and breathing exercises. There's also dance—Sufi whirling dervishes—as well as the martial arts: karate, kung fu, tai chi.

Meditation teachers suggest meditating at the same time every day—even if it's only for five minutes. The length of your meditation time, most say, is less important than the opportunity to train your mind through daily practice. Establishing rituals such as lighting a candle or incense or ringing a bell at the beginning of your practice helps you switch gears into contemplative mode.

Sitting quietly, doing nothing
Spring comes, and the grass grows by itself.

—ZENRIN, *THE GOSPEL ACCORDING TO ZEN*

To write this chapter, I made plans to observe a silent retreat at an abbey deep in the barren, rocky hills of northern Colorado. Won't that be wonderful? I thought. No kids, no e-mail, no phone—no distractions. I'll just meditate and focus on this writing task. As the date approached, though, I realized I was terrified. I'd never spent a full twenty-four hours without uttering a word. I panicked at the thought of not being able to escape into my favorite CD when the writing got hard. What if I needed to talk to my children?

While perhaps not life changing, the retreat was definitely enlightening. Most important, I discovered how loud and distracting my daily life really is. I've been known to pull a smug holier-than-thou because my TV doesn't get any channels, but I seek solace from my own emotions in bluegrass and jazz—played very loudly—and the telephone. I doubt I could pull off an entire week in silence at this point, but twenty-four hours of it gave me a means of understanding my own noise.

In his classic treatise on meditation, *Journey of Awakening,* Ram Dass writes about his own personal transformation from a music junkie—with tunes constantly blaring in his car and throughout his home (even in the bathroom)—into a quiet epicurean. "I found that I was beginning to appreciate the silence and was content to enjoy a few pieces of music or art thoroughly rather than fill every space with sound and with imagery," he writes.

You don't have to become Ram Dass to quiet your lifestyle. You can start with some very simple baby steps. Leave the television off for one night a week. Turn off the radio during your morning commute, turning the drive into a time of quiet preparation for the day

138

ahead. Practice a few moments of silence before eating a shared meal. Make time in the afternoon for a quiet cup of tea.

A couple of years ago, I visited the home of Sarah Susanka, the architect who wrote *The Not So Big House* and has spearheaded the not-so-big-house movement. In keeping her home as small as possible, Sarah designed it so that most of the rooms serve several different needs: the bathroom is also the dressing room, the TV is tucked away in a corner of the living room. But one room served just one person and a very specific need; that room was Sarah's meditation space in the attic.

Sarah said she agonized, at first, over whether to include this seemingly self-centered room. She also knew that she desperately needed a space where she could escape. So she created the attic meditation space, painted it a deep, contemplative red, and brought in her favorite books, candles, and incense. She's never looked back.

"If you make a place like this, with the intention to make time to use it, wonderful things can happen," Sarah told me. And indeed, Sarah is now the author of four books and the leader of a movement that's changing the way Americans look at their homes. She claims none of that would have been possible if she hadn't had a place to connect with quiet.

Do you have a space in the attic or maybe a small spare bedroom where you can create a room dedicated to quiet and solitude? Ideally, this space would have a door so that you could close it off, assuring yourself privacy. Consecrate this as your personal space in which to find peace. Eventually, the vibes you leave in there will

I would like you, even in this busy age and even though your house may be small, to set aside a space (although it may seem a wasteful use of space) to serve as a place where you can reflect upon yourself. . . . When it is time to retire at night, roll up the scroll, just as you would change into your nightclothes, and place it within the alcove, toward the side. When you rise in the morning, you can hang the scroll again with refreshed feeling. Although it is the same scroll, this will bring out its freshness and the significance of hanging it in the alcove.

—SEN SOSHITSU XV

accumulate, and simply entering the space will begin to prepare your mind for meditation.

Giving yourself a space to meditate may seem like a luxury, especially if you live in tight quarters. It may even be downright impossible—and that's okay. Simply designate a quiet corner in your bedroom or even living room as your meditation space. Keep a rug or a mat that you can unroll there when you want to meditate. (While you're unrolling the rug, concentrate on creating a sacred space and changing the room's atmosphere.) Hang a meaningful piece of art on the wall—perhaps one that represents peace and spiritual abundance to you. On a small table in this corner, keep incense, candles, and other meditation tools. If your private space is in a public spot and you're not comfortable having others see these things, find a table with a drawer or store them in a pretty box.

If you're lucky enough to have a separate room you can dedicate to meditation, it's a great place to start developing your wabi-sabi sensibilities. The basics of a meditation space are simple: a cushion or a straight-back seat for sitting and a small table to hold candles, an incense burner, a photo or statue of someone who inspires you, and perhaps some helpful meditation or poetry books. You also might want to bring in a plant or seasonal flowers, a picture of yourself in a relaxed, joyful state, bells or singing bowls, and a stone or branch from one of your favorite natural hangouts. Buddhist altars generally include the five offerings to the deities: incense, flowers, water, sandalwood powder, and fruit or cooked rice. You can follow this tradition or create your own offerings.

Personally, I like to keep as few electronic devices in my meditation space as possible; I don't like the buzzy energy they bring to the space. But I have friends who swear by meditation tapes and CDs (there's an infinite variety on the market these days, from guided meditations to music), so they keep a CD player in the room. I also know people who have created their own tapes by ringing a chime at the beginning, waiting the desired amount of meditation time, then ringing the chime again to signal the close of meditation. This can really help if you tend to be a clock watcher.

If you're extremely sensitive to noise and have the resources, consider soundproofing this one room in your house. Raising the floor, dropping the ceiling, building double walls, and installing a sealed door will run you at least an extra $50 a square foot, so it may be easier (and it will definitely be cheaper) to just locate your meditation room in the quietest part of your house.

In the spirit of wabi-sabi, keep this room as simple as possible. Western spiritual guru Ram Dass suggests that plain, bare walls are most conducive to meditation. If you'd rather soften the walls with fabric or color, stick to soft, subtle, muted tones. Spend time looking for an altar table that you truly love—perhaps an antique—and if possible, try out several different meditation cushions to find the one most comfortable for you. If the room doesn't have a window, hang a photo of an inspiring natural scene—whether this is a grove of birch trees, a vast canyon, or ocean waves is entirely up to you.

141

## A ROOM OF ONE'S OWN

In most family homes, kids get their own rooms (and sometimes playrooms besides), yet parents are expected to share their bedroom and den. Only those who work at home are allowed private space—and that's for commerce, not relaxation.

There's no place in the modern American home, it seems, for grown-ups to call their own—even though most experts now believe it's crucial to healthy family dynamics. "We need privacy even when we're married," clinical psychologist Alvin Baraff told the *Washington Post* more than a decade ago, "to maintain separate interests and identities; otherwise resentment builds."

We need to claim a private space in our homes—and it doesn't necessarily have to be a meditation room. Maybe it's your own little corner for morning coffee, where you feel safe and unhindered while writing in your personal journal. Maybe it's a craft room—not just a place to store wool and needles, but a place that fosters creativity. Here you can display your favorite projects or the work of others that inspires you. You can keep a bulletin board with scribbled quotes and magazine pictures you like. You can bring in that totally comfy armchair that's way too threadbare for public consumption, and you can have it all to yourself (and your knitting needles). You can paint the walls any color you like—whether that's brown (which your husband calls "drab") or bright purple. It's *your* room, and you can do what you want.

• This is the room of no compromise. Always wanted to live in a genie bottle? Paint the room in jewel tones and stuff the perimeters with cushions. Who cares if others find this weird? No one else is supposed to see it, anyway. Feel like writing on the walls, or lining them with pebbles or shells? Do it. Want to make sure no one joins you? Make sure there's only one comfortable place to sit.

If you only have one extra room in your house, curtain it down the middle so you and your spouse can each have a share. Even if you live alone, designate a space that's off limits to visitors. The key is to commit, wholeheartedly, to giving yourself room to grow.

Hedonistic? Perhaps. And this isn't necessarily a bad thing. Because we can't hone our wabi sensibilities—knowing as we do that the crux of it is learning to appreciate solitude and stillness—if we can't ever be alone in our own homes.

Perchance the time will come when every house even will have not only its sleeping-rooms, and dining room, and talking room or parlor, but its thinking room also, and the architects will put it into their plans. Let it be furnished and ornamented with whatever conduces to serious and creative thought.

—HENRY DAVID THOREAU

# Chapter 6

# practice makes imperfect

# release

For many of us, interior design magazines and books are food for neurosis. We can't help ourselves from diving into those seductive, glossy pages, marveling over the stylish, expensive rooms—so finished, so perfect. Everything is considered and carefully placed, down to the art books poised on the tufted ottoman and the flawless calla lilies leaning just so against the sides of a sparkling crystal vase. Could these homeowners be parents? They've obviously found a more stringent means than you or I of keeping their kids from bringing bowls of chocolate ice cream into these living rooms. Could this home include pets? If so, they are hairless.

All things are literally better, lovelier, and more beloved for the imperfections which have been divinely appointed.

—ART CRITIC AND ESSAYIST
JOHN RUSKIN

145

Having directed photography shoots for many years, I know what often lurks outside the frames of these shots. It takes a crew of us to create a picture-perfect room. We move out the evidence of daily life—the piles of receipts, paperback novels, and prescription bottles on bedside tables—and we pull in Andy Goldsworthy books and sake sets. We spend hours placing furniture, fixing fringe, and plumping pillows. We pore over Polaroids before the final shot, checking for fatal flaws such as exposed electrical cords and crooked lampshades. "Wait, wait!" someone will cry, before the photographer presses the shutter. She'll rearrange the folds of the draperies, and everyone will nod with satisfaction. Thank *God* she saw that!

But most people see these photos and believe that real people actually live this way. And we can't help it—we're struck with feelings of unworthiness. Our homes will never look like these, with their sleek, dry-martini living rooms and plush, draperied boudoirs. We never even got around to hanging curtains in a couple of rooms, and the stains in the carpet just seem to magically reappear within days after it's been cleaned. Unlike those magazine homeowners, we have appliances—toaster ovens and clock radios and other ungainly plug-in things—and they clutter up our surfaces. Our candles melt funny, our throws don't drape, and when we try artfully leaving a few lemons out on the kitchen table, it just looks like we didn't put all the groceries away.

Then comes the confusion. Are we really so shallow? Do we really believe it would change our lives for the better if we could fold fitted sheets and make military-style beds? Is hot-gluing fabric borders onto our lampshades really the best use of our time? Do we have it in us—and do we want it?

Then comes the guilt. Aren't we snobs for not displaying the granny-square afghan our mother-in-law crocheted for us? Isn't it hideously materialistic of us to want a $1,400 lamp—when that amount could house a few homeless families for a month? We really should be content just to have a roof over our heads . . . shouldn't we?

We become locked in the struggle between envy and repulsion; our inhuman drive for perfection and our human need for comfort. We do want beautiful, nurturing homes, but we don't want to succumb to the price of entry and the constant maintenance that perfection demands. We want our kids (if not the dog) to feel welcome on the living room sofa, and we don't want to find ourselves plugging in the Dirt Devil every hour on the hour. We want to invite guests into a clean, hospitable home, and we want to learn how to be okay with it if they put their glass down on the coffee table without a coaster.

What we really crave is not material gloss but comfort. We want a place where we can slow down and revel in the texture of our lives, our histories unfolding. A place where our kids' lumpy pottery class projects (or our own) are not out of place. A place where scratches in the hardwood floor are a cherished reminder of the dog's later days—not flaws to be ashamed of. We don't want a showcase; we want a home.

Learn to let go.
That is the key to
happiness.

—BUDDHA

148

My sister Stacey used to help remodel high-end homes in Santa Monica. She got to spend oodles of the clients' money on Viking stoves and granite countertops, designer paint and custom cabinetry. When she was finished, the homes were fresh and stunning. Yet during the final walk-through, the clients would inevitably pick out every nick in the woodwork, every scratch in the floor. Try as she might to explain that the house would be covered with little dings within six months of their moving back in, she could rarely get the clients to calm down. They'd just spent all this money on a renovation, and they wanted their house to be *perfect*. "We would go back a few months later to take photographs, and sure enough, the baseboards would be all smudged and the refrigerator full of fingerprints," she says. "And what would you expect? These people *live* there."

There's a certain seduction in a brand new or newly renovated home—or even just a fresh coat of paint. No marks or flaws, no signs of human wear. Photo ready. Perfect.

You can maintain that level of perfection if you want to be a Felix Unger, constantly cleaning and scrubbing, following people as they move through your house with a rag and a bottle of cleaning spray. You can keep an inhospitable plastic cover on your sofa and make people wear those little booties over their shoes when they visit. You can always be alert for errant fringe and sloppily folded towels. Maybe you already do this. Have you counted the hours you spend futzing and plumping? Are you having any fun?

✗ Psychologists tell us that keeping our homes immaculate is a means of trying to wrest control in an unpredictable, uncontrollable world. War, famine, and crime may plague the outside world, but damn it, our kitchen sink sparkles! And in fact, we've also been brainwashed from the time we were infants (housework being one of the first activities we all witnessed) to believe that our ability to keep a clean, neat house is a direct correlation to how much we love and care for our families.

We live in a society that values—even demands—perfectionism (the perfect ten, a perfect match, perfect teeth). Yet in our homes, this perfection standard was set for a generation much different than our own, one where the threat of profound poverty was very real and a dirty, disheveled home was the ultimate symbol of that disgrace. Advertising blossomed as this generation came of age, and it exploited these fears. As magazine and newspaper advertising revenues tripled from 1918 to 1929, American housewives were inundated with not-so-subtle messages that the way they kept house was a direct reflection on their values and their love for their family. Laundry was an expression of love; cleaning the bathroom protected the family from disease. What kind of housewife wouldn't attack these tasks with all the vigor she could muster?

There have been voices of dissent, of course—and from surprising sources. In the late nineteenth century, domestic doyenne Catherine E. Beecher was alarmed by the number of women she met who seemed to be overwhelmed by their domestic duties. She advised them to make a list of all the things that needed to get done, figure out what they just could not do, then strike those off the list. "You will have the comfort of feeling that in *some* respects you are as good a housekeeper as you can be," she wrote in *American Woman's Home, or, Principles of Domestic Science*, published in 1869.

Christine Frederick, who popularized home economics in the early twentieth century, was also aware of the toll these impossibly high standards were taking on women. Houses should not be run according to "arbitrary standards, set up by friends or the community," she wrote in *Household Engineering: Scientific Management in the Home* in 1919. She advised women to keep their homes according to "whatever methods conduce to the efficient management of her particular home, regardless of tradition, or what is supposed to be the 'proper' way."

We are all, to some extent, ruled by "shoulds" and "have tos." We "have to" keep a spotless bathtub (or germs will grow); we "should" change the sheets every week (to kill the dust mites). That kind of black-and-white thinking, however, takes away our freedom and kills all the joy in keeping house. Remember the hundred shades of gray found in Japanese kimono? The same holds true with our housekeeping standards—we can learn to define success on a continuum. Unless you have severe allergies, changing the sheets every nine or ten days instead of every seven is not going to kill you or your family members. (Not making the bed every day won't kill you either, despite what your mother might have taught you.) Yes, a clean bathtub is important, but sanitizing it every day is just not necessary. In fact, breathing in the fumes from commercial tub and tile cleaners every day can be much more damaging to your health than a few germs. Letting go of absolute rules and living in the gray zone will make your life much more manageable and peaceful. Remember the old motto "My house is clean enough to be healthy and dirty enough to be happy."

Traditional gardeners in Japan—a society where high standards of cleanliness and precision are revered even more than in our own —keep absolute perfectionism at bay by scattering handfuls of leaves over their garden paths once their work is done. American quilters used to make it a habit to hide an imperfection in their work, a flaw that perhaps only they could find. And during those magazine photo shoots, once we've painstakingly hidden all the electrical outlets, the stylist will sweep in and shake a few rose petals loose or sprinkle a few kernels of popcorn next to the bowl. We will all nod with satisfaction. These little moments of imperfection make all the difference.

151

Back in the nineties I was married, briefly, to a wealthy man in New York. We made residence in a *fabulous* Tribeca loft wrapped in terra-cotta baked in Italy and adorned with chic velvet furnishings and big-name art. Some people (somewhat snidely, I now realize) called it a palace. The living-room floor was a marble masterpiece, and copper gleamed throughout the house. The Austrian crystal was paper thin; the French bed linens soft and thick.

I hated living there.

The price of entry for my cat, Babe, was her claws; they were

It is neither wealth nor splendor, but tranquillity and occupation, which give happiness.

—THOMAS JEFFERSON

removed after she sharpened them on the spiral-shaped red velvet sofa—which looked a lot like a scratching post to me, too. Poor Babe was never quite the same again. I got to keep all my body parts, but I did feel like I forfeited a lot of creature comforts to live in that house. I was always nervous, constantly on guard against my own natural clumsiness—everything was priceless and must not be broken. I gave up cooking; it made such a mess of the white-on-white kitchen. Taking a bath really wasn't worth leaving water-marks on the deep copper tub. The living-room furnishings were sculptural and hip, made by famous designers, but I never could find a comfortable place to while away the afternoon with a book. Once some old friends of my parents', Jack and Nancy, came to spend the night, and Jack was hit with insomnia. "Why don't you just go sit in the living room?" his sleepy wife suggested. "Because there's no place to *sit* in there," he hissed. Another friend called it a "museum-cum-residence," and it truly was more Met than home.

A decade later, my "palace" would have been viewed as a peasant's hovel compared with the imperial taste of chief executives that has come to be known as mogul style—homes filled with ridiculous extravagances such as $6,000 shower curtains and $15,000 umbrella stands. As the century turned, contemptuously spending huge sums for household luxuries became the ultimate ego game for the rich and famous.

Perhaps the need to spend exorbitant sums on household luxuries is an attempt to compensate for an inexplicable emptiness within. We Americans, after all, have been programmed to believe that if something's not right, throwing money at it is always a good

For Buddhists, worshiping the beautiful—or perfect—and hating the ugly—or imperfect—is considered immature. If all of life exists on a continuum, and everything in our world is interrelated, Buddhism teaches, then this antagonism can't be real.

Zen Buddhists view the entire universe as one's own true self, believing that heaven, earth, and humans all grew from the same root. Therefore, the natural order includes things that are beautiful and ugly, sweet and bitter, happy and sad—all aspects of life and everything in between. When we learn to look at life this way (and that can take a lifetime), imperfection, decay, and death all become much easier to accept—and life becomes much easier to live.

Although everything has Buddha nature, we love flowers and we do not care for weeds. . . . A flower falls, even though we love it, and a weed grows, even though we do not love it.

—DOGEN-ZENJI

solution. One of my favorite Texas songwriters, Guy Clark, tells us that there's only two things that money can't buy: true love and homegrown tomatoes. His lyrics fall short, though. Money can't buy soul, and it can't buy comfort. In fact, both are more likely to be found in humble surroundings.

Kind of brings us right back to those warlords who ruled Japan back in Sen no Rikyu's day, doesn't it? Toyotomi Hideyoshi and his gold-leaf tearoom would have fit in quite well with the wealthy upper crust of corporate America. But for all the gaud and ostentation, Hideyoshi's tearoom couldn't hold a candle to Rikyu's small thatched hut. An invitation to have tea in the simple, rustic environment Rikyu created was much more coveted.

154

*

The great depend
on their heart,
not on their purse.

—RALPH WALDO
EMERSON

Think about the things in your home that you love best. Perhaps they're very-expensive-recognize-the-designer pieces, but if you've read this far, my guess would be they're not. They're the things that hold more meaning than a designer name and reveal more about you than how much money you have to spend—your collection of books, a basket full of seashells you collected on your honeymoon, the clock that once hung in your grandmother's parlor. These are the things that interior designer Ruby Ross Wood referred to as "the pleasant memorabilia of living." They break the crust of superficiality and dive into the soul.

In my house, these things include two Shaker-style tables and a secretary that my father made; always my favorite pieces of furniture, they've taken on even more meaning for me since he died. I remember my father spending hours down in his basement shop

My dad made this table
out of hand-planed
cherry wood. It's a daily
reminder of his love and
his fine craftsmanship.

when I was young, working miracles on a fine piece of cherry wood with his saws and chisels. I think of him every time I oil the silky smooth surface of the coffee table, bringing out the golden striations of the wood he so meticulously sanded. I hear his voice every time I open one of the drawers on his sofa table, so proud of how smoothly and effortlessly it glides open—without any extraneous hardware. There's not a furniture store in the world where I could buy that.

I'm fortunate that my dad was a fine craftsman, but almost everyone has an heirloom or two—or even just hand-me-downs or cast-offs—that hold memories. These could be linens that your grandmother embroidered or the beanbag ashtray your grandfather always had by his side. Maybe you still have the jewelry box you received from your parents for your tenth birthday or the tablecloth that graced your great-aunt's Thanksgiving table. Whatever it is, value it, take care of it, and try to find a spot in your home to honor it. It doesn't matter if the linens are stained or the ashtray is irretrievably tarnished. Evidence of wear over the years is a reminder of the loved ones who used these things—proud wabi-sabi markings.

Next time you visit an older relative, ask to see family photographs—and get the stories behind them. My mom had dozens of sepia-toned portraits in a box in her garage; just before my dad died we went through them together, and he was able to tell me who was who—and then some. Do I really believe that Parker fellow was a cousin of Bonnie and Clyde? I might have my doubts, but it sure makes for good conversation. I brought home a handful of photos, and I've been collecting old-fashioned frames for some of my favorites: my grandmother as a saucy young flapper, my mother as a cherubic three-year-old, my dad's handsome hand-tinted senior portrait. Grouped on a shelf in my dining area, they look great, and they're a daily connection with my ancestry.

Take a look around your house. Can you tell a story about most of the objects you see? None of us can, or should, be expected to have *only* family heirlooms or folk art we picked up on our travels —wabi-sabi's not supposed to be about setting limits, after all. But do you find that the majority of your home decor reflects your interests, your uniqueness? If not, think about how you can start injecting yourself into your home—even in small ways. Replace canned art with an enlarged photo from your last vacation, or frame one of your children's paintings. Build shelves so you can surround yourself with the books you love. Make a rag rug (or have it made) out of clothes your kids have outgrown. Spray your pillow with your favorite scent. Keep your favorite music on the CD player, and remember to turn it on.

157

Pressing flowers behind glass is a simple project that also lets you bring nature inside. There's nothing to it—just find the blossoms you like, place them within a frame, and replace the glass. These mosaic tile frames are also an easy DIY project.

Without personal touches, a home is just a house. I was at a photo shoot recently in Berkeley, in a home that was up for sale. In the bizarre game of California real estate, the current trend is to remove every trace of the homeowners and pay a "stager" to come in and deck the house for viewing. The home was lovely, dripping with tasteful furnishings and objects, all perfectly placed. Bland classical music played on a continual loop. We hardly had to do a thing to prepare each room to be shot—the stager had even left open books with reading glasses and breakfast trays complete with fake food on the beds. Yet all the fun was gone. With the home-owner's imprint stripped away, we might as well have been shooting stage sets for a catalog. No favorite blanket to drape over the sofa, no heirloom teacups, no quirky artwork. No life. Just perfection.

158

. . . the lust for comfort, that stealthy thing that enters the house a guest, and becomes a host, and then a master.

—KAHLIL GIBRAN

Where do you go when the world's got you down? Do you have at least one place in your home that welcomes you with open arms, a place that invites you to snuggle in? Do you have a favorite chair—one so soft and nurturing that you couldn't bear to part with it? Is there an ottoman or a hassock nearby so you can put your feet up? Does everyone in your household have a soft blanket or quilt to wrap themselves in when they watch TV?

In our quest for decorating perfection, we too often overlook comfort—the most important matter of all. We order designer sofas from catalogs without ever testing their springs. We load our beds with shimmery silk throw pillows that were never meant to be rested on. We banish the threadbare armchair—even though it's the most comfortable seat in the house.

The most aesthetically exciting hotel room I've ever stayed in was also the most sensually miserable. Modernist, spare, and streamlined, it had no place to store an extra blanket, so I shivered through the night under the thin white bedspread. The concrete floors were trendy, but first thing in the morning they were cold and uninviting to my bare feet. The lighting seemed harsh and brilliant, with nothing soft to absorb it. After an uncomfortable forty-eight hours, I decided I'd trade in tragically hip for the staid pleasures of a closet shelf with an extra blanket and a bedside rug.

What makes a room comfortable? A soft seat or two. A sofa you can sink into. Slipcovers, which lend an air of impermanence.

159

When it comes to textiles, age and wear add valuable character. Frayed, faded textiles bring wabi-sabi energy into any space.

Gentle lighting. A subtly textured rug. A place to set your teacup. Windows that open wide.

Basic stuff, you say? Start paying attention to how many rooms you walk into that lack most—or even all—of these things. Maybe your own living space could use one or two of these touches. Consider covering your sofa pillows in a gingham that fades. Turn off harsh overhead lamps and light candles. Replace inoperable windows with double-hungs or casements. Sit down in every chair in your house; is there a place nearby to rest a book and a cup? Sleep in your own guestroom and ask yourself if you've provided everything your guests need for a comfortable stay. Make sure there's an extra blanket.

Have you ever noticed that when someone gives you a tour of their home, they inevitably point out a few flaws? That outdated light fixture needs to be replaced; the kitchen layout is completely inconvenient. They wish they'd chosen a different shade of green for the bathroom. Some day, they sigh, some day maybe their home will be perfect.

For years, I wallowed unhappily in my own home's many imperfections and offered them all up to anyone who would listen. Certainly my little house isn't anyone's dream home—it's simply the best we could afford in a town where housing prices are insane. The picture window in the living room is an ugly metal thing. The bathrooms are tiny and poorly designed. The vinyl on the kitchen floor was an unfortunate choice. The yard has a mind of its own. I couldn't get myself motivated to do anything about all these indig-

160

Everything has its wonders, even darkness and silence, and I learn, whatever state I may be in, therein to be content.

—HELEN KELLER

nities because I believed the solution was to move, to start over again somewhere else. But the years ticked by, we stayed where we were, and eventually I got tired of hating where I lived.

✳ My house lacks many things. I wish it had a formal dining room. I wish the windows were made of wood. I wish it had a deep, winding front porch. But it has a few things going for it, too. Two wise, strong maple trees flank the east and west corners, providing welcome shade in summer and strong arms for my daughter's swing and my son's treehouse. My bedroom window offers a dramatic mountain view. In winter, when a fire in the woodstove is enough to heat both upstairs and down, it's a snug and cozy place. It's not such a bad little house.

As long as we dwell on our home's negative aspects, we will never find peace. The first step in creating a wabi-sabi home that nurtures the soul is simply an attitude adjustment. Instead of focusing on all that's wrong in your home, make a serious attempt to find everything that's good. You can even go as far as making a list of all your home's positive points; I suspect you'll be surprised to find that they far outweigh its detriments. Try to remember why you moved into this house in the first place—surely there were good reasons. Perhaps the location is ideal. Do your kids have friends in the neighborhood? Maybe it was simply all you could afford—there's a lot to be said for not living beyond your means (that's actually very wabi).

✳ Put this list of positive aspects up in a place where you will see it often, and the next time you curse the inadequate lighting in the entryway or the leaky single-pane windows on a frosty morning, read it again. Recite it out loud if you need to.

Next, go ahead and make a list of improvements you'd like to make—everything from new knobs for the kitchen cabinets to french doors in the den. The key here is to make this a positive, not a negative, endeavor. This isn't about how horrible the current knobs are, but an optimistic vision of what they could be. Maybe you'll get around to these next week, or maybe in a year or two. It doesn't matter. This is all an exercise in attitude and intention—the most crucial building blocks to a happy home.

God, grant me the serenity to accept the things I cannot change; courage to change the things I can; and wisdom to know the difference.

—REINHOLD NIEBUHR, "THE SERENITY PRAYER"

On my desk I keep a mug with this saying: "Peace. It does not mean to be in a place where there is no noise, trouble, or hard work. It means to be in the midst of those things and still be calm in your heart." The first time I tried to pour coffee into this mug, it seeped out through a small hairline crack in the bottom and spilled all over the countertop. Our daily lives are rife with imperfections. We can let these wriggle inside our heads and make us crazy, or we can accept this as the way it is—even find the amusement in them. And we can practice this acceptance most often—and to most effect—at home.

So your home's exterior paint is starting to alligator. The wood floors need a good sanding. The windows are full of streaks. All of these things can be really annoying, if you let them. But if you were told today that you had two weeks to live, would you make it a priority to rush home and address them? "Kids, I love you," you might say. "And I'd really love to spend these last two weeks with you. But I'd sure hate to leave behind these scratched-up floors."

I came face to face with my own perfection complex a couple of years ago as I made frantic last-minute preparations for our annual Christmas Eve party. I always make too much food and stay up deep into the night on December 23 trying to make the house look . . . well, perfect. I wanted Christmas Eve to be a magical experience for my kids and my guests, with lights twinkling, a table groaning with food, a visit from Santa. But by 4 p.m. on the day of the party, I was angrily searching for the coconut while swiping at the baseboards (why hadn't I noticed before how *filthy* they were?) and arranging evergreen boughs for the table. "Mommy, will you play with me?" my daughter Cree, bored and unhappy, kept asking again and again. "When can you play with me?"

163

"I can't play with you," I answered. "Can't you see how much I have to do? I haven't even set the table yet. And don't crack those nuts in here!"

Cree burst into tears. "Mommy, I hate the Christmas Eve party!" she said. "I hate Christmas Eve!"

Devastating. I sank down onto the floor, leaned against the dirty baseboard, and took my daughter into my lap. We pulled up the bowl of nuts and, together, cracked them and threw the shells on the floor. As the afternoon light dimmed, we lit candles and saw that by their flickering light no one would ever know that our house wasn't spotless. No one seemed to miss the coconut in the appetizers, either. In fact, more than one person commented on how calm and relaxed our house felt, that it was the best Christmas Eve party we'd ever had.

I'd like to say that I never succumbed to a perfection frenzy again, but that would be a lie. All too often I feel like I can't rest until the floors have been scrubbed or the garden beds weeded. I've been known to take a vacuum cleaner to the lava rocks flanking the patio, desperate to remove the leaves that accumulate there. But I've also learned that I can live with less-than-spotless baseboards if it's a choice between staying home to clean them and attending my son's hockey game.

In the end, it all comes down to priorities. Allow yourself a few moments to get familiar with yours.

164

After all, what is your hosts' purpose in having a party? Surely not for you to enjoy yourself; if that were their sole purpose, they'd have simply sent champagne and women over to your place by taxi.

—P. J. O'ROURKE

For many of us, it seems, the worst of our neuroses come bubbling to the surface when it comes time to entertain. Even if every one of our guests is a close friend who's seen our house at its absolute worst, we feel compelled to make it spotless for this event, to wow them with our culinary skills, and to live up to the image of the mostest hostess—that mythical figure we all believe we should be —that lives inside our heads.

How many parties have you gone to where everything, down to the personalized napkin holders, was *perfect*—except for the host and hostess, who were fried and frenzied? You see these parties featured in magazines: theme parties with cute centerpieces made out of baseball mitts, crystal and china place settings for twenty, little pumpkins with each guest's name carved in them. Hey, I've been to a few of these photo shoots, and you know what? It takes even more people to stage these sets than it does a house shoot. And that happy hostess and her smiling guests? They're *models*. They're being paid for those smiles.

But we all drool over these articles; they appeal to the grandiosity buried deep within us. And the insecure side of us thinks that maybe if we send our guests home with personalized Christmas tree ornaments, they'll like us more. We'll be more popular. Probably not, though. When I leave a party where everything's catered and coordinated and it seems like the host has been cooking and preparing for days, I think, "I can never have that person to one of my parties. What would she think of me?"

The thing is, themes and centerpieces aren't what make a good party—people do. And if you're completely exhausted from cooking, cleaning, and cutting out place cards with pinking shears, you'll never be able to enjoy the guests you brought together. And your guests, taking their cue from you, will never relax and appreciate each other.

Think about some of the gatherings that you've most enjoyed in your life: impromptu popcorn parties in your dorm room, marshmallows roasted over a fire on the beach, an eclectic potluck, chili and cocoa after sledding. The beauty in these events was that no one felt the need to be in charge, no one felt responsible. It was about company, not control. It was simply about having fun and enjoying the mix of people who came together.

Simple, more relaxed entertaining doesn't mean you have to serve hot dogs on paper plates. Never give up on the idea of honoring your guests by preparing elegant, seasonal fare and presenting it as beautifully as possible. But there's a distinct difference between trying to please and trying to impress. So simply stop and think about your motivations. If you have plenty of time on your hands and are itching to get creative, by all means make a home-made piñata and hollow out coconut shells to serve drinks in. But if you really just want to celebrate the summer solstice and haven't had time to prepare, invite guests for lemon cake and sorbet in the backyard—and simply encourage everyone to soak up the longest day of the year. Chances are, they'll be happy to gather with others to mark the day; they probably won't even notice that you didn't have time to string little lanterns over the patio.

The most important thing you can do as a wabi-sabi hostess is to pay attention to your guests' every need. Serve a variety of food so that everyone's diet—from vegan to Atkins—is covered. If it's cold, greet guests with a hot drink and invite them in to a room warmed by a roaring fire. If it's warm, play tropical music and pass out fans. Keep their drinks filled. Watch for wallflowers and spend as much time as you can with them. Introduce guests to one another and stick around to spark conversations. First and foremost, bear in mind Sen no Rikyu's seventh rule of tea: Always be mindful of the guests. They're your first, your last, your everything.

## THE CANDLE TRICK

So, you come home at the end of a long day and the dog's been on the sofa again and the breakfast bowls are still full of dried oatmeal and the entry hall *still* needs a coat of paint. All you want to do is relax and let go of the cares of the day—enjoy a little stillness and solitude in your home. But who can rest in this mess?

Try this very simple solution. Throw the dishes in the sink to soak and throw a blanket over the sofa. Turn out all the lights. Take a match to two or three candles, placed strategically away from the dirty dishes and the dog hair so that their light pools only on empty space. Relax. Nothing looks quite so bad when the atmosphere is dim and flickering.

Chapter 7

wabi-sabi balance

# accept

I was deep into my research on wabi-sabi, learning all there is to know about simple, humble living, when my husband announced that we needed a new TV. Fair enough, I agreed, our old set was a twenty-year-old hand-me-down from my parents. Off he went to one of those home-entertainment super-stores, and home he came with a fifty-five-inch high-definition set—and a new DVD player that matched its capabilities. I was mortified. Anyone who peeked into the room where the machine and all its accom-panying wires and speakers is set up would immedi-ately identify me as a wabi-fraudie. How could I live with this hulking symbol of Western excess right here in my own home?

If this is the best of all possible worlds, what are the others?

—VOLTAIRE

Thing is, the sound and the picture can't be beat. After years of fuzzy color and tinny voices, the big, flat screen and the surround sound really do feel luxurious. Snuggling in with a bowl of popcorn and a film we never got to catch at the theater makes for a really nice Saturday night. I eventually had to admit, grudgingly, that I *like* this horrible thing. I am not a wabi-sabi purist. God help me.

I am undoubtedly a victim of crass consumer culture—a citizen of this material world. I'll never live up to the noble ideals of wabi-sabi as practiced in a more idyllic time and place. I fall victim to the catalogs that arrive at my door every day and the semiannual Nordstrom sale, where I get to practice what my favorite shoe salesman refers to as "spaving," a combination of spending and saving. I've spent astonishing amounts on custom-fit curtains and used the word "need" in association with household luxuries. Thoreau would be appalled.

This is our imperfect world, and it's littered with commercial land mines. Every day, it seems, we're hit with another electronic gadget that will make our lives easier, more productive, more meaningful. In the past decade we've been convinced that we can't live without microwaves, personal computers, handheld organizers, and cell phones. High-end furnishings dripping with bland, universal good taste are available to everyone at the local mall (the one with all the same stores as the local mall in the next town over . . . and the next . . . and the next). And that mall is no longer a mall; it's a "retail resort." Shopping is entertainment. Just ask your teenaged daughter and her friends.

We all know the price we're paying for these burgeoning amenities. We're working harder and longer than ever before. We can't possibly stop for a cup of tea while the e-mails pile up and the orders are coming in. During the year it took to pay off that big TV set, my husband and I actually had time to sit down and watch a movie on it less than a dozen times. Opinion polls consistently find that most Americans believe they buy and consume far more than they need and that they'd be happier if they could spend more time with family and friends. Why don't we, then?

Thorstein Veblen coined the term *conspicuous consumption* way back in 1899. His theory was that people buy things to show everyone else who—and how wealthy—they are. Members of each social group see what the class above them is buying and try hard to get those things, too. Thus, the cycle we know as "keeping up with the Joneses" (or better yet, leaving the Joneses behind) continues on and on.

While academics often criticize Veblen's theory as too simplistic, most also have to admit that he was onto something. At the turn of the century, Veblen was observing a society that had just leapt over the brink toward industrialism and global distribution capabilities; more stuff was available to more people in more places than ever before. At the same time, more people were moving from rural areas into the cities, leaving behind the roots by which they'd identified themselves. They filled the holes left by the family and community they no longer had with readily available—and

To found a great empire for the sole purpose of raising up a people of customers may at first sight appear a project fit only for a nation of shopkeepers.

—ADAM SMITH,
*THE WEALTH OF NATIONS*

extremely seductive—consumables. The trend steamrolled for the next century—and here we are today. Per capita consumption in the United States jumped by 45 percent from the 1970s to the 1990s; we represent 5 percent of the world's population and consume nearly 30 percent of its resources.

Women, especially, have been programmed to believe in the power behind their buying power—in fact, in certain eras that may have been the only power they really had. By the 1920s, savvy shopping and acquiring had become the hallmark of a good homemaker. "Most of us are becoming more and more convinced that a principal function of home economics instruction is to train for the wise selection of and utilization of household goods," stated a *Journal of Home Economics* editorial in 1927. By the turn of the next century, not all that much has changed. "The ugly side of consumerism exists because there is something deeply meaningful about shopping," sociologist Dan Cook told *The Christian Science Monitor* in 2002. "Shopping is the provisioning of care, and the marketplace brings social intercourse and cultural interchange."

We shop; therefore we are. We work so we can shop. This is the reality of living in today's Western civilization.

172

What if everything is an illusion and nothing exists? In that case, I definitely overpaid for my carpet.

—WOODY ALLEN

So, how do we find our wabi-sabi way in this overwhelmingly consumerist culture? We can join the growing numbers of Americans who are taking part in the voluntary simplicity movement, paring down their commitments and possessions to buy more time and freedom. These folks are proving that simple living is not only possible but also can be infinitely more fulfilling than the rat race.

But not all of us are there yet. We know we're not satisfied with life in what philosopher Jean Baudrillard calls the "simulcrum"—the Disney-like world of overconsumption—yet we're also not quite ready to chuck it all and go live a monklike existence in the woods. We find ourselves in a sort of wabi-sabi never-never land.

Don't we *have* to take vows of poverty and live in mud huts to truly practice wabi-sabi? Of course not. The truth is, most of the men who brought wabi to the forefront of Japanese culture in the sixteenth century weren't living that way. Sen no Rikyu made a fine living selling his highly sought-after rustic tea wares and bamboo vases, and these days wabi aficionados part with exorbitant sums to acquire his originals. Wabi became the aesthetic of the Japanese upper crust, just as the wabi-influenced arts-and-crafts movement shaped the design of American robber barons' summer cottages centuries later.

If we spend our time dwelling on all that's wrong with our over-stimulated consumer culture, our anger and despair will do nothing but get in the way of our desire for change. Yep, we buy too much stuff. Yep, we're using way more than our fair share of the world's resources. We could easily convince ourselves that these are fatal flaws in our collective culture and that we'll never get this wabi-sabi thing. But I know that a wabi spark exists in many Americans—I've heard it, seen it, and felt it as I've published articles and conducted workshops on the subject across the country. People who see the need for change—but are also tired of being hit over the head with all the guilt associated with their lifestyles—suddenly have an "aha" moment when they discover wabi-sabi.

They've found a guiding philosophy toward positive, gentle change. And the best thing about it is its emphasis on imperfection. There is no such thing as perfect wabi-sabi.

What we must learn to do—and this is no easy task—is to adapt the spirit of wabi-sabi and apply that to our daily lives. We can do this aesthetically through clean, uncluttered design and simple, rustic furnishings and decor. We can meditate or at least allow ourselves five quiet minutes each day. Maybe we can learn to work with clay, knit our own dishtowels, or grow a few herbs in the kitchen windowsill. These are all important steps. But we also need to make a mental shift, to stop seeing ourselves primarily as consumers. Can we start seeing ourselves in our intentions, our actions, and our relationships—not in what we buy?

If we had more time than money, how would we change our own lives and those of our families and our communities? What if we eliminated one half hour of shopping each week and spent it instead with family and friends? What if we spent as much time and attention maintaining and repairing our household goods as we do buying new ones? This seems simplistic until you add up the hours you spend on each and compare them. Bet you'll be amazed.

Sometimes you'll make frivolous—or at least not entirely necessary—purchases. But as you develop a wabi-sabi mind-set, you'll be more likely to stop and ask yourself whether you really need something before you rush out to buy it. Could the old sofa be slipcovered rather than replaced? Could you share a lawn mower with the neighbors instead of buying your own? Could you live with a few chips in the soup bowls?

In the late 1990s, photos of artist and filmmaker Julian Schnabel's Greenwich Village apartment—described by one designer as "hyper-decayed, totally rotting"—appeared in *Vogue*. Dank and moldy, with exposed pipes full of rust, tattered curtains, and ancient, splintery furnishings, the place might have been construed as the ultimate in wabi-sabi design. Except for one thing. Those two words—*ultimate* and *wabi-sabi*—just don't work together in the same sentence. Schnabel's apartment was too much statement, another ploy from an artist famed for his attention-getting antics. There was nothing subtle or beautiful about it, and you certainly wouldn't want to *live* there.

Here lies a danger in embracing wabi-sabi with too much force—the difference between wabi-sabi and wabi-snobby (or Schnabel's expensive form of slobby-wabi-snobby). Too much wabi-sabi is simply too much.

We Americans love to take things to superficial extremes, and we also have an unfortunate tendency toward quick fixes. We've done this with herbal medicine; instead of drinking herbs in tea form, which forces us to slow down and let the healing move subtly through our systems, we've isolated the plants' properties into poppable pills and tinctures. We've done it with *feng shui*; Chinese masters are appalled at our hang-this-crystal-and-get-yourself-a-boyfriend mentality. It would be so easy to rush out and buy ourselves a room full of wabi-sabi—distressed, even decaying, furniture is everywhere these days. We could look down our noses at anything new, sleek, or high-tech—refuse to allow these things into our homes. But that wouldn't necessarily make us into wabibito.

You will express yourself in your house whether you want to or not. . . . We attribute vulgar qualities to those who are content to live in ugly surroundings.

—ELSIE DE WOLFE,
*THE HOUSE IN GOOD
TASTE*, 1913

175

Some day—maybe even some day soon—you'll start scouring salvage yards and flea markets for wabi-sabi furnishings. Some day—maybe even some day soon—you'll clear all the clutter out of your living space. In the meantime, you'd like to start bringing wabi-sabi into your home and into your life right now. You can start by taking these simple, basic steps. You'll be amazed at the difference they can make.

**ONE DAY A WEEK, WASH THE DINNER DISHES BY HAND.** Taking on this task alone allows you quiet, uninterrupted time to think—or not think. Asking your spouse or child to help gives you time to catch up on each other's days.

**PAY ATTENTION TO YOUR DAILY BREAD.** Is the food you're eating in season, and is it available locally? Through the meals you prepare, you can connect with the earth's cycles and with the place where you live—and live a healthier life. Buy food from your local farmer's markets and ask the produce manager at your grocery store where different items came from.

**OPT FOR THE BROOM** over the Dirt Devil whenever possible. Next time you sweep the floor, consider it a meditation.

**BRING A SMALL GIFT** when you're invited to someone's house, nothing extravagant, just a small gesture (a jar of homemade jam or apples from your tree, perhaps) that lets them know they're appreciated.

**OFFER EVERYONE WHO COMES TO VISIT A CUP OF TEA.** Serve it in pretty cups with a little something sweet. If no one comes by, enjoy a cup of tea by yourself in the late afternoon.

**KEEP ONE VASE IN YOUR HOME FILLED** with seasonal flowers.

**TAKE A WALK EVERY DAY.** Let this be your opportunity to open up your senses and to experience the changing seasons.

**LEARN TO KNIT** or crochet.

**STOP AND ASK QUESTIONS** next time you buy something. Who made it? How was it made? Where does it come from?

177

Wabi-sabi is about restraint. It's about trusting our own intuition and developing our understanding of moderation. One or two decrepit pieces add character and charm—even register a subtle note of protest against our modern world—but a whole room full is extreme. Remember tea master Murata Shuko's refrain: "It is good to tie a praised horse to a straw-thatched house." Combining wabi-sabi design elements with more traditional decor will only serve to highlight both.

My hat has come apart
during a long journey.
I am a wabi man who
has tried and know
every wabi thing.

—MATSUO BASHŌ,
FROM *WINTER DAYS*

For far too many of us, home—decorating it, maintaining it, keeping up with it—all too often represents stress. Every day the catalogs and magazines arrive, bearing photos of finished, tasteful houses. We can't help but want those tasteful interiors and gorgeous gardens, but we're also stretched to the limit just trying to keep the floor swept and the clutter contained. When home improvement projects eat up our weekends, we stop appreciating where we live—the natural wonders unique to our geographies and the strength of our communities. We forget how lucky we are to have a roof over our heads and a warm bed to sleep in.

When wabi-sabi philosophers refer to "the joy of the little monk in his wind-torn robe," they're reminding us to let go of the superficial and pay attention to the simple, everyday pleasures of being alive. Maybe we should keep the little monk in our minds the next time we decide we *need* a new sofa or contemplate putting ourselves in debt to furnish the dining room. Will these things make us happier? Or will the new sofa call for a new lamp, a new coffee table, a new shade of paint, and another lost weekend? Will we enjoy our food more on a brand new dining table? Or could we instead spend the working hours required to buy it preparing and presenting lovelier, more thoughtful meals? There's no right or wrong answer, of course. These are just questions the little monk might ask.

The little monk reminds us of our mortality, the impermanence of our life here on this earth. We all know that at the end, we won't look back and say, "I sure wish I'd found time to tile the bathroom." We might, however, look back and regret that we didn't stop to play soccer with the kids because we were too busy tiling the bathroom. Let go, the little monk whispers softly. Let go of the need for more, the desire for perfection, the insatiable appetite. Wrap your wind-torn robe around you and take a seat in your favorite, worn armchair. Just be. And in this moment, you will know wabi-sabi. And to know wabi-sabi is to know peace.

179

## LIVING RIGHT NOW: A ZEN LESSON

Kichibei was a common villager whose wife's illness kept her bedridden. Every day, in addition to caring for his wife, he had to cook, sweep, and clean his home. One day a neighbor remarked that he must be exhausted.

"I do not know what fatigue is," Kichibei replied, "because caring for my wife every day is always both a first experience and a last experience. There is no doing it again, and so I never tire of it."

## resources

The following listings of both information resources and companies that sell related items will aid in your journey to learn more about creating a wabi-sabi environment at home. These resources were incredibly helpful to me, but they are meant to serve only as guidelines and starting points. To find your own wabi-sabi way you will likely want to search for your own sources, especially when you shop for home furnishings.

### CHAPTER 1: "WHAT IS WABI-SABI?"

The Urasenke Foundation, www.urasenke.or.jp/texte/index.html, offers instruction and information about the way of tea through several locations worldwide. In the United States:

URASENKE CHANOYU CENTER
153 East 69th St.
New York, NY 10021
(212) 988-6161

URASENKE HAWAII
245 Saratoga Rd.
Honolulu, HI 96815
(808) 923-1057

URASENKE SAN FRANCISCO
2143 Powell St.
San Francisco, CA 94133
(415) 433-6553

URASENKE SEATTLE
1910 37th Place East
Seattle, WA 98112
(206) 324-1483

URASENKE WASHINGTON
6930 Hector Rd.
McLean, VA 22101
(703) 748-1685

### CHAPTER 2: "GIVE SPACE A CHANCE"

CLUTTERLESS RECOVERY GROUPS
www.clutterless.org
A nonprofit organization run by clutterers, for clutterers.

GOODWILL INDUSTRIES INTERNATIONAL
9200 Rockville Pike
Bethesda, MD 20814
(240) 333-5200
www.goodwill.org
Collects your unwanted clothing and household goods.

NATIONAL ASSOCIATION OF PROFESSIONAL ORGANIZERS
35 Technology Parkway S., Ste. 150
Norcross, GA 30092
(770) 325-3440
www.napo.net
hq@napo.net

### Web sites
www.beclutter-free.com
www.FlyLady.net

### CHAPTER 3: "YOU'VE GOT THE LOOK"

#### Antiques
INDIANA'S ANTIQUE ALLEY
www.antiquealley.us
(800) 775-3928

KOVELS ONLINE
www.kovels.com
An online antique and collectibles reference.

#### Finishes: Floors, Walls, Windows
FLOORING
BARNSTORMERS FLOORING
166 Malden Tpke.
Saugerties, NY 12477
(845) 246-3622
www.safesolutionsllc.com
Flooring, furnishings, and cabinets made from recycled barn wood.

EARTH WEAVE CARPET MILLS
P. O. Box 6120
Dalton, GA 30722
(706) 278-8200
www.earthweave.com
Hemp and wool carpet.

ECO-FRIENDLY FLOORING
100 S. Baldwin St., Ste. 110
Madison, WI 53703
(866) 250-3273
www.ecofriendlyflooring.com
Bamboo, cork, recycled glass tile, stone, reclaimed wood.

ECO TIMBER
(888) 801-0855
www.ecotimber.com
Antique and reclaimed flooring.

LYONS TILE
15493 King Ranch Road E.
Odessa, WA 99159
(509) 982-2182
www.lyonstile.com

THE NATURAL CARPET
COMPANY
(310) 447-7695
www.naturalcarpetcompany.com
info@naturalcarpetcompany.com
Natural fiber carpets: raffia,
wool, wood, bamboo, seagrass.

NATURAL CORK
1710 N. Leg Ct.
August, GA 30909
(706) 733-6120
www.naturalcork.com
info@naturalcork.com

**PAINTS, PLASTERS, AND
FINISHES**
AGLAIA NATURAL PAINTS
(800) 322-6843
www.aglaiapaint.com

BIOSHIELD
(800) 621-2591
www.bioshieldpaint.com
info@bioshieldpaint.com
Clay paints and plasters,
natural pigments.

CLAYOTE EARTH PLASTER
American Clay
(866) 403-1634
www.americanclay.com

THE NATURAL FINISH
(888) 256-4821
www.thenaturalfinish.com
Natural oils, stains, paints,
waxes.

THE OLD FASHIONED MILK
PAINT COMPANY
(978) 448-6336
www.milkpaint.com

TERRAMED
(866) 363-6334
www.medimports.net
info@medimports.net
Natural clay plaster.

**RUGS**
WOVEN LEGENDS
4700 Wissahickon Ave.
Philadelphia, PA 19144
(215) 849-8344
www.wovenlegends.com
Naturally dyed, handmade
carpets from handspun wool.

**WALLCOVERINGS**
CDS MANUFACTURING
441 S. Virginia St.
Quincy, FL 32351
(850) 875-4651
www.cdsmanufacturing.net
Cast stone for cornices,
moldings, and walls.

JADECOR
(888) 677-3642
www.jadecor.com
Natural cotton wallcovering.

**WINDOW TREATMENTS**
EARTHSHADE
(413) 528-5443
www.earthshade.com
Natural window coverings.

## Furniture
**CHARLES AND RAY EAMES**
EAMES OFFICE GALLERY
2665 Main Street, Ste. E
Santa Monica, CA 90405
(310) 396-5991
www.eamesoffice.com
info@eamesoffice.com
Furniture, Eames films,
photographs, links, and
information on visiting the
Eames house.

HERMAN MILLER
855 East Main Ave.
P.O. Box 302
Zeeland, MI 49464-0302
(888) 443-4357
www.hermanmiller.com

**DANISH**
EUROPEAN FURNITURE
IMPORTERS
2145 Grand Ave.
Chicago, IL 60612
(800) 243-1955
www.eurofurniture.com

SCANDINAVIAN DESIGN
Box 7090 S.E.-200
42 Malmo, Sweden
46 (40) 92 92 00
www.scandinaviandesign.com

181

## HANDCRAFTED WOOD FURNITURE

BERKELEY MILLS
2830 Seventh St.
Berkeley, CA 94710
(510) 549-2854
www.berkeleymills.com
Asian, arts-and-crafts style
furnishings.

DANKO/PERSING ENTERPRISES
214 N. Franklin St.
Red Lion, PA 17356
(800) 882-5300
www.peterdanko.com
Tables and chairs made from ply-bent wood (in Eames tradition).

FOUND WOOD FURNISHINGS
6142 Hillegass Ave.
Oakland, CA 94618
(510) 594-1905

GARY WEEKS
112 West Spoke Hill Rd.
Wimberley, TX 78676
(888) 334-0307
www.garyweeks.com
Handmade wood furniture.

NATURAL TREE FURNITURE
436 Ave. H
Wilson, KS 67490
(785) 658-2618
www.smithindustries.com

SLEEPYWOOD RUSTIC FURNITURE
1552 Duckwall Rd.
Berkeley Springs, WV 25411
(304) 258-9549
www.sleepywood.com

## MIDCENTURY MODERN

R 20TH CENTURY
82 Franklin St.
New York, NY 10013
(212) 343-7979
www.r20thcentury.com
r@r20thcentury.com

### Web sites
www.designaddict.com (go to links and select "vintage")
www.jetsetmodern.com
www.midcenturyandmodern.com

### THOMAS MOSER
THOS. MOSER CABINETMAKERS
P.O. Box 1237
Auburn, ME 04211
(877) 708-1973
www.thosmoser.com
Thomas Moser designs are in five showrooms across the country: Freeport, Maine; New York City; San Francisco; Charleston, South Carolina; and Chicago. For directions and information, go to www.thosmoser.com/showrooms.htm.

### GEORGE NAKASHIMA
GEORGE NAKASHIMA WOODWORKER, S.A.
1847 Aquetong Rd.
New Hope, PA 18938
(215) 862-2272
www.nakashimawoodworker.com
info@nakashimawoodworker.com
Catalog, tours of Nakashima's studio(by appointment only),

ordering information for new furniture, and *Nature, Form and Spirit* by Mira Nakashima, (Harry N. Abrams) can be ordered here.

MODERNE GALLERY
111 North 3rd St.
Philadelphia, PA 19106
(215) 923-8536
Exhibits, information about and sales of vintage Nakashima furniture.

## NATURAL MATERIALS
EL: ENVIRONMENTAL LANGUAGE
425 Park Barrington Drive
Barrington, IL 60010
(847) 382-9285
www.el-furniture.com
Natural, nontoxic, elegant furniture.

FURNATURE
86 Coolidge Ave.
Watertown, MA 02472
(800) 326-4895
www.furnature.com
Natural, nontoxic furniture, reupholstering, slipcovers, window treatments, and cushions.

KORQINC
155 E. 56th St.
New York, NY 10022
(212) 758-2593
www.korqinc.com
Cork furniture.

UKAO GRASS FURNITURE
3644 San Gabriel Lane
Santa Barbara, CA 93105
(805) 563-3100
www.ukao.com
Furniture made from bamboo,
bio-based textiles, and stone.

**RECYCLED FURNITURE**
PLANET SQUARED
PO Box 3944
Huntington Beach, CA 92605
(714) 846-0650
www.planetsquared.com
Environmental art and recycled
furniture.

RESOURCE REVIVAL
2267 N. Interstate Ave.
Portland, OR 97227
(800) 866-8823
www.resourcerevival.com
Furniture made from recycled
bicycle parts.

TIFFANY TOMATO DESIGNS
539 S. 5th Ave., Studio 1
Ann Arbor, MI 48104
(734) 347-7849
www.tiffanytomato.com
Housewares made from garbage
—and some great DIY projects.

**SALVAGED AND RECLAIMED
WOOD FURNITURE**
AIREDALE WOODWORKS
307 N. Second St.
Murfreesboro, NC 27855
(800) 489-0639
www.airedalewoodworks.com
Furniture made with wood
from old tobacco barns.

ROBERT BRANDEGEE DESIGNS
2250 Mary St., Apt. 301
Pittsburgh, PA 15203
(412) 488-7046
www.robertbrandegeedesigns.com
Furniture made with wood
from old log structures.

RUSTIC FURNITURE OF MOAB
76 S. Main #14
Moab, UT 84532
(435) 259-4457
www.rusticfurnitureofmoab.com
Furniture made with wood
from old barns, houses, fences
and sheds.

WHIT MCLEOD
P.O. Box 132
Arcata, CA 95518
(707) 822-7307
www.whitmcleod.com
Arts-and-crafts furniture built
using reclaimed and salvaged
wood.

THE WOODEN DUCK
2919 Seventh St.
Berkeley, CA 94710
(510) 848-3575
www.thewoodenduck.com

## Salvage
**HABITAT FOR HUMANITY
RESTORES**
More than 50 Habitat for
Humanity affiliates across the
United States and Canada have
established ReStores, which sell
used and surplus building
materials donated by
contractors, demolition crews,
and the general public.

To find a ReStore near you, go
to www.habitat.org/env/
restore.html.

HABITAT FOR HUMANITY
INTERNATIONAL
121 Habitat Street
Americus, GA 31709
(229) 924-6935, ext 2551
publicinfo@hfhi.org

USED BUILDING MATERIALS
ASSOCIATION
1702 Walnut St.
Boulder, CO 80302
(303) 440-0703
www.ubma.org

## Web sites and publications
Resources for finding and using
natural furnishings and finishes

NATURAL HOME MAGAZINE
201 E. 4th St.
Loveland, CO 80537
(970) 669-7672
www.naturalhomemagazine.com
Natural home and lifestyle
magazine.

www.environmentalhome
    center.com
www.abundantearth.com
www.ecochoices.com
www.envirointeriors.com
www.home-environment.com
www.whitelotus.net
www.eco-furniture.com
www.antiquarius2000.com
www.ecosofa.com
www.ecodesignresources.com
www.environmentaldepot.com
www.salvageweb.com

183

## CHAPTER 4: "HANDS ON"

### Handmade Goods

CHISTA
537 Greenwich Street
New York, NY 10013
(212) 924-0394
www.chista.net
Innovative furniture, tribal and
primitive objects.

EZIBA
120 Mass MoCA Way
North Adams, MA 01247
(888) 404-5108
www.eziba.com
Items from global sources.

NOVICA.COM
(310) 479-6685
www.novica.com
Representing artisans from
around the world.

TEN THOUSAND VILLAGES
704 Main St.
Akron, PA 17501
(717) 859-8100
www.tenthousandvillages.com
Handicrafts from Third World
artisans.

### Craft Museums

MINGEI INTERNATIONAL
MUSEUM
1439 El Prado
Balboa Park
San Diego, CA 92101
www.mingei.org
mingei@mingei.org

MUSEUM OF INTERNATIONAL
FOLK ART
706 Camino Lejo
Santa Fe, NM 87505
www.nmoca.org/
mnmfolkart.html

NIPPON MINGEIKAN
Japan Folk Craft Museum
4-3-33 Komaba, Meguro-ku
Tokyo
(03) 3467-4527

SHUNPU BANRI SO
Village of the Art
1371 Shimo-Ichige
Kasama-City, Ibaraki
0296-72-0958
Traditional home of Japanese
potter Kitaoji Rosanjin.

### Web sites and publications

INTERWEAVE PRESS
201 E. 4th Street
Loveland, CO 80537
(970) 669-7672
www.interweave.com
Magazines and books related to
fiber, thread, needlework, and
beads.

READYMADE MAGAZINE
2706 Eighth St.
Berkeley, CA 94710
www.readymademag.com
"A magazine for people who
like to make stuff."

www.churchofcraft.org
www.craftychica.homestead.com
www.craftygalcom
www.ehow.com
www.eknitting.com
www.getcrafty.com
www.knitandcrochet.com
www.learntoknit.com
www.stitchguide.com

## CHAPTER 5: "THE SOUND OF SILENCE"

NOISE FREE AMERICA
P.O. Box 15620
New Orleans, LA 70175
(504) 488-6800
www.noisefree.org
director@noisefree.org

THE NOISE POLLUTION
CLEARINGHOUSE
P.O. Box 1137
Montpelier VT 05601-1137
(888) 200-1137
www.nonoise.org
npc@nonoise.org
A nonprofit dedicated to
creating more civil cities and
more natural rural and
wilderness areas by reducing
noise pollution.

WORLD FORUM FOR ACOUSTIC
ECOLOGY
http://interact.uoregon.edu/
MediaLit/WFAE/home/
index.html

Baldwin, Billy. *Billy Baldwin Decorates* (Secaucus, NJ: Chartwell Books, 1972).

Berendt, Raymond D., Edith Corliss, Morris Ojalvo. *Quieting in the Home,* reprinted from National Bureau of Standards Handbook 119 (Washington, D.C.: U.S. Environmental Protection Agency Office of Noise Abatement and Control).

Bethel, Dayle M. *Makiguchi The Value Creator: Revolutionary Japanese Educator and Founder of Soka Gakkai.* (New York: Weatherhill, 1973).

Browning, Dominique, and the editors of *House and Garden Magazine. House & Garden Book of Style: The Best of Contemporary Decorating* (New York: Crown Publishing Group, 2001).

Conran, Terence. *Easy Living* (San Francisco: Bay Soma Publishing, 1999).

Csikszentmihalyi, Mihaly, and Eugene Rochberg-Halton. *The Meaning of Things: Domestic Symbols and the Self* (Cambridge: Cambridge University Press, 1990).

Dal Co, Francesco, editor. *Tadao Ando: Complete Works* (London: Phaidon Press, 1995).

Dass, Ram. *Journey of Awakening: A Meditator's Guidebook* (New York: Bantam Doubleday Dell, 1990).

Elgin, Duane. *Voluntary Simplicity: Toward a Way of Life That is Outwardly Simple, Inwardly Rich* (New York: William Morrow and Co., 1993).

Frederick, Christine. *Household Engineering: Scientific Management in the Home* (Chicago: American School of Home Economics, 1919).

*George Nakashima and the Modernist Moment* (Bucks County, PA: James A. Michener Art Museum, 2001).

Glassman, Bernard, and Rick Fields. *Instructions to the Cook: A Zen Master's Lessons in Living a Life That Matters* (New York: Bell Tower, 1996).

Kapleau, Roshi Philip. *The Three Pillars of Zen: Teaching, Practice, and Enlightenment.* (New York: Knopf Publishing Group, 1980).

Kirkham, Pat. *Charles and Ray Eames: Designers of the Twentieth Century* (Cambridge, MA: The MIT Press, 1998).

Koren, Leonard. *Wabi-Sabi for Artists, Designers, Poets and Philosophers* (Berkeley: Stone Bridge Press, 1994).

Leavitt, Sarah A. *From Catherine Beecher to Martha Stewart: A Cultural History of Domestic Advice* (Chapel Hill, NC: The University of North Carolina Press, 2002).

Moore, Thomas. *The Re-Enchantment of Everyday Life* (New York: HarperCollins, 1997).

Moser, Thomas F., with Brad Lemley. *Thos. Moser: Artistry in Wood* (San Francisco: Chronicle Books, 2002).

Nakashima, George. *The Soul of a Tree: A Woodworker's Reflections* (Tokyo: Kodansha International, 1981).

Okakura, Kakuzo. *The Book of Tea* (New York: Dover Publications, 1964).

Soshitsu, Sen. *Tea Life, Tea Mind* (New York: Weatherhill, 1979).

Soshitsu, Sen XV, *The Spirit of Tea* (Kyoto: Tankosha Publishing Co., 2002).

Suzuki, Daisetz T. *Zen and Japanese Culture* (Princeton, NJ: Princeton University Press, 1959).

Suzuki, Shunryu. *Zen Mind, Beginner's Mind: Informal Talks on Zen and Practice* (New York: Weatherhill, 1977).

Tenshin, Okakura. *The Book of Tea* (Tokyo: Kodansha International, 1998).

Thoreau, Henry D. *Walden, or Life in the Woods* (Boston: Ticknor and Fields, 1854).

Thoreau, Henry D. *The Portable Thoreau* (New York: Penguin, 1976).

Torniainen, Minna. *From Austere Wabi to Golden Wabi: Philosophical and Aesthetic Aspects of Wabi in the Way of Tea* (Helsinki: Studia Orientalia, 2000).

Warner, Jisho, Shohaku Okumura, John McRae, and Taigen Dan Leighton, editors. *Nothing Is Hidden: Essays on Zen Master Dogen's Instructions for the Book* (New York: Weatherhill, 2001).

Wellwood, John, editor. *Ordinary Magic: Everyday Life as Spiritual Path* (Boston and London: Shambhala, 1992).

Wilde, Oscar. *Essays and Lectures by Oscar Wilde* (London: Methuen and Co., 1908).

*The Work of Charles and Ray Eames: A Legacy of Invention* (New York: Harry N. Abrams, 1997).

Yanagi, Soetsu, *The Unknown Craftsman: A Japanese Insight into Beauty* (Tokyo: Kodansha International, 1972).

In addition to interviews with tea masters, artists, art critics, and others, a good deal of information came from former *House Beautiful* editor Elizabeth Gordon's papers—an extensive collection of articles, correspondence, and photographs related to her study of shibui—which are available for viewing at the Freer Gallery of Art and Arthur M. Sackler Gallery Archives, Smithsonian Institution, in Washington, D.C.

Page 9. "The essence of education . . ." Tsunesaburo Makiguchi, in *Makiguchi The Value Creator: Revolutionary Japanese Educator and Founder of Soka Gakkai*, 1973.

Page 17. "The Japanese view of life . . ." Tadao Ando, in *Tadao Ando: Complete Works*, 1995.

Page 18. ". . . active aesthetical appreciation of poverty," D.T. Suzuki, "Zen and the Art of Tea I," The University of North Carolina at Chapel Hill web site, www.unc.edu.

Page 19. "Enduring poverty in life . . ." Matsuo Bashō, in *From Austere Wabi to Golden Wabi*, 2000.

Page 20. "Things fall apart . . ." W.B. Yeats, "The Second Coming," 1921.

Page 22. "Long life is not gained from wealth. . . ." Buddha, *Pali* canon (ancient text).

Page 23. "The peculiar dilemma . . ." Anthony West, "What Japan has that we may profitably borrow," *House Beautiful*, August 1960.

Page 34. "The earth is designed . . ." Sparrow, "Autumn Now," *The Sun*, December 2001.

Page 37. "A person who has not found . . ." Jo-o, in *From Austere Wabi to Golden Wabi*, 2000.

Page 43. 300 pages of paper . . . 25 percent more furniture . . . "De-junking your home," *Health Diary*, Spring 1999.

Page 43. We . . . use about 20 percent of our stuff . . . Julie Morgenstern on "Fresh Air," National Public Radio, December 7, 1998.

Page 43. "Tangible clutter is anything . . ." Harriet Schechter, "From Chaos to Comfort: Unclutter Your Home, Your Head and Your Heart," SoulfulLiving.com, October 2002.

Page 45. "We live in a cluttered world . . ." Dr. Jerold Pollack, in "Culture of clutter: Healthy Living: Collecting stuff—for good or ill," *The Atlanta Journal and Constitution*, January 22, 2002.

Page 46. "It makes us emotionally comfortable . . ." psychologist Marsha Sauls, in *The Atlanta Journal and Constitution*, January 22, 2002.

Page 53. "If you like to collect things . . ." Tyler Brule, "Less is more...but where do you put your stuff?" *Independent on Sunday*, February 2, 1997.

Page 53. ". . . a pared-down approach to domestic life . . ." Dominique Browning, *A House & Garden Book of Style*, 2001.

Page 53. ". . . every day you have to spend time . . ." John Pawson, "The lure of minimalism: Intriguing yet frightening, this style is the latest status symbol," *The Minneapolis Tribune*, January 2, 1997.

Page 53. "There's no stopping them . . ." John Pawson in "At Home: Objects of desire," *Independent on Sunday*, May 13, 2001.

Page 54. "I cannot help but feel . . ." Terence Conran, *Easy Living*, 1999.

Page 55. "I hate to sound like my mother . . ." Brian Carter in "The lure of minimalism: Intriguing yet frightening, this style is the latest status symbol," *Minneapolis Star-Tribune*, January 2. 1997.

Page 55. "In Mies there is something tragic . . ." Tadao Ando, in *Tadao Ando: The Complete Works*, 1995.

Page 65. "If you can't find beauty . . ." and "You have to wipe away all judgments . . ." Elizabeth Gordon, in *House Beautiful*, May 1958.

Page 66. "I find that what your people need . . ." Oscar Wilde, *Essays and Lectures by Oscar Wilde*, 1908.

Page 68. "For if a man cannot . . ." Oscar Wilde, from *Essays and Lectures by Oscar Wilde*, 1908.

Page 68. "A bird, a butterfly, a spider . . ." Thomas Moser, *Thomas Moser: Artistry in Wood*, 2002.

Page 70. "There is a cachet now in dust. . . ." Min Hogg, in "Don't Chuck Out Your Chintz . . . , *Independent on Sunday*, February 16, 1997.

Page 75. "The essence of this look . . ." Wendy Lubovitch in "Everything old is new again; Flea market furnishings give a room one-of-a-kind look and feel," *Minneapolis Star Tribune*, August 17, 2000.

Page 75. "I was astounded by . . ." Tadao Ando, in *Tadao Ando: The Complete Works*, 1995.

Page 76. "Everything made by man's hands . . ." William Morris, "The Decorative Arts, Their Relation to Modern Life and Progress," an address to the Trades' Guild of Learning, Dec. 4, 1877, at www.burrows.com.

Page 76. "The purpose is usefulness . . ." George Nakashima, *The Soul of a Tree*, 1981.

Page 77. "Fundamentally, I have a primary interest . . ." George Nakashima, "Nakashima's Solution: His Own Woodworking," *New York Herald Tribune*, October 25, 1953.

Page 78. "The perfect piece of furniture . . ." Thomas Moser, *Thos. Moser: Artistry in Wood*, 2002.

Page 80. "It is alive..." Tibor Kalman, in *The Work of Charles and Ray Eames: A Legacy of Invention*, 1997.

Page 87. "The Babel of modern color . . ." Jed Perl, "Colors," *The New Republic*, March 4, 2002.

Page 87. "Be restrained rather than overluxurious . . ." William Morris, from an address delivered to students of the Birmingham Municipal School of Art, www.marxists.org.uk/archive/morris/works/tmp/birm_art.htm

Page 91. "Handmade things, with all their wonderful . . ." Faith Popcorn, in "Celebrity Knitters . . . Look Who's Knitting!" by Trinity, www.worldknit.com.

Page 92. "So many things in life . . ." M. Joan Davis in "Tending to Their Knitting; An Old Needle Art Wins New Converts," *Washington Post*, March 28, 2002.

Page 93. "My life is worthwhile . . ." Callie Janoff, cofounder, Church of Craft, *11211 Magazine*, Vol. 2, #3.

Page 96. "Fortunately people are artists . . ." W.R. Lethaby, "Art and Workmanship," *The Imprint*, January 1913.

Page 98. "The ideal home life today . . ." Christine Frederick, in *Household Engineering*, 1919.

Page 99. "Machine-made things . . ." Soetsu Yanagi, *The Unknown Craftsman*, 1972.

Page 105. "Handcraftsmanship, if it be alive . . ." Bernard Leach, in *The Unknown Craftsman*, 1972.

Page 105. "The owner acts with it . . ." Kiki Smith, "Gallery Discussion/Kiki Smith and Robin Johnson," November 15, 1999, www.daiichiarts.com/lectures.asp.

Page 107. "Japan has four seasons . . ." Okita Matsuura, in "Rosanjin's Views on Cookery," http://www.tsuji.ac.jp/hp/jpn/jp_e/kanazawa/5.htm.

Page 109. "Just cultivate delight . . ." Diane Ackerman, interview on National Public Radio's *Talk of the Nation*, June 7, 2002.

Page 111. "If you fiddle . . ." Sen Soshitsu XV, *The Spirit of Tea*, 2002.

Page 119. ". . . in undisturbed solitude and stillness . . ." Henry David Thoreau, *Walden, or Life in the Woods* (Boston: Ticknor and Fields, 1854).

Page 120. "Calling noise a nuisance . . ." Dr William H. Stewart, in "The Path to Quiet: Don't Just Say 'No' to Noise—Say 'Yes' to Quiet," by Nancy B. Nadler, *Hearing Rehabilitation Quarterly*, Volume 25, No. 1, 2000.

Page 123. "The ears are the most intimate . . ." Thomas Moore, *The Re-Enchantment of Everyday Life*, 1997.

Page 124. "Noise abatement ranks right up there . . ." Norman Remich, in "Quieter Kitchens: Tips for Lowering the Boom on Noise," *Home Mechanix*, November 1992.

Page 132. "To my mind, the idea . . ." Thich Nhat Hanh, "Sunshine and Green Leaves," in *Ordinary Magic: Everyday Life as Spiritual Path* (Shambhala, 1992).

Page 139. "I would like you . . ." Sen Soshitsu XV, *The Spirit of Tea*, 2002.

Page 142. "We need privacy . . ." Alvin Baraff, in "Retreats: A Room to Call One's Own: The Boundless Need for Personal Space," *Washington Post*, April 4, 1991.

Page 143. "Perchance the time will come . . ." Henry D. Thoreau, "A Yankee in Canada," in *The Portable Thoreau*, 1976.

Page 172. "The ugly side of consumerism . . ." Dan Cook in "You want it, you buy it, you forget it; A new exhibit explores the evolution of our shopping habits and uses art to delve into what drives us to shop, consume, and shop more," *Christian Science Monitor*, December 5, 2002.

Page 175. "hyper-decayed, totally rotting . . ." M. Scott Marks, in "Rusticated (Consumed—the 'rustic' look in fashion and decoration)," *The New Republic*, April 3, 1995.

Page 175. "You will express yourself . . ." Elsie de Wolfe, in *Billy Baldwin Decorates*, 1972.

Page 178 "My hat has come apart . . ." Matsuo Bashō, quoted from *The Winter Days* on NTTWest Shizuoka web site, www.shizuoka.isp.ntt-west.co.jp.

187

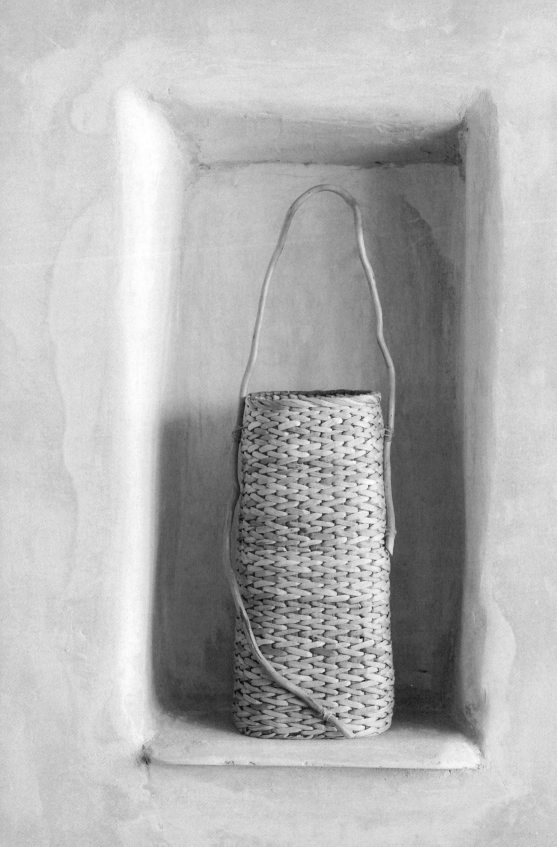

## acknowledgments

I owe a huge debt to my husband, Matt, and my kids, Stacey and Lucretia, for their patience and understanding throughout this process. Thanks also to my mom, Suzanne Griggs, who's put up with (and even encouraged) my tell-all nature since I learned to write in first grade; to my boss, Linda Ligon, who graciously allowed me breathing space and opened up her home for photographs; to my agent, Elyse Cheney, who saw that America was ready for wabi-sabi and never gave up on it; to the nuns at St. Walburga Abbey and to Ann and Preston Browning of Wellspring House, who provided quiet, sublime writing spaces; to my friend and guardian angel in Japan, Linda Nicita; to all the teachers at Bikram Yoga on Baseline, without whom I never would have made it through this. Thanks to my first editor, Annetta Hanna, who understood wabi-sabi from the start and helped me see how to translate it, and to my second editor, Jennifer DeFilippi, who picked up the ball with enthusiasm and terrific vision. Thanks also to the many people who so generously gave of their time and wisdom, including Larry Tiscornia, Christy Bartlett, Gary Cadwallader, Shiho Kanzaki, Junji Ito, Kyoko Mimura, and Colleen Hennessey. And last but not least, Kate NaDeau, for introducing me to wabi-sabi in the first place.

189